Thinking Robots, An Aware Internet, and Cyberpunk Librarians

The 1992 LITA President's Program

Presentations by Hans Moravec, Bruce Sterling, and David Brin

LITA Pres

D1089533

R. Bruce Miller and Milton T. Wolf, Editors

Library and Information Technology Association
Chicago, Illinois 1992

Printed on 50-pound acid-free Finch Opaque and bound in 10-point CIS cover stock by IPC, St. Joseph, Michigan.

The paper used in this publication meets the minumum requirements of the American National Standard for Information Sciences—Permanence of Paper for Printed Library Materials, ANSI Z39.48-1984.∞

Publication design and page preparation by Walt Crawford using the facilities of the *LITA Newsletter.* Produced using Ventura Publisher Gold (GEM Edition), Hewlett-Packard's LaserJet III, Pacific-Page XL PostScript emulation, and Pacific Type typestyles. All typefaces from Bitstream, Inc.

This book is set in Goudy Old Style, with titles, section headings, and section footings set in Futura.

Library of Congress Cataloging-in-Publication Data

Thinking robots, an aware internet, and cyberpunk librarians : the 1992
    LITA president's program : presentations by Hans Moravec, Bruce Sterling, and David Brin [et al.] / R. Bruce Miller and Milton T. Wolf, editors.
      p.   cm. — (LITA president's series)
    Includes bibliographical references and index.
    ISBN 0-8389-7625-5
    1. Libraries—Automation—Congresses. 2. Information technology—
Congresses.
    I. Moravec, Hans P. II. Miller, R. Bruce (Robert Bruce), 1946– .
    III. Wolf, Milton T. IV. Library and Information Technology Association (U.S.) V. Series.
Z678.9.T46 1992
025′.00285—dc20   92-30742
                                                CIP

Contents

Why Should I Read This? (And Who Are These People, Anyhow?)

R Bruce Miller

University of California, San Diego

"You've done it, and something like this can't be undone. Like the start of the nuclear age, way back when. You can't stuff it back into the box and tell Pandora you'll get back to her when you're more ..." the senator shrugged "... more 'moral,' to use the quaint terminology. So if we can't undo it, we'd better have as much control over it as possible."—Pat Cadigan, *Synners*. (New York: Bantam, 1991) 136.

~~~~~~

This is about values.

This is about myriad and amazing possibilities.

This is about shared vision.

The Program

The President of the Library and Information Technology Association for 1991/92, Paul Evan Peters, dreamed of this program for years. The 1992 LITA President's Program, *Tools for Knowing, Environments for Growing: Visions of the Potential of Information Technology for Human Development*, was the fulfillment of that dream. The program was developed by the LITA Imagineering Interest Group (more about them later). The brilliant futurists, Hans Moravec, Bruce Sterling, and David Brin, expanded the vision of the audience as they moved beyond the use of technology solely for the automation of text and the mechanization of information processing to

1

encompass a future in which the relationships between humans and their information machines will be distinctly personal and symbiotic.

- **HANS MORAVEC** is a world renowned roboticist. His book, *Mind Children: The Future of Robot and Human Intelligence*, presages the "downloading" of the human brain into robotic bodies. His presentation, "Pigs in Cyberspace" postulates a future in which robots have urbanized matter, space, and time.

- **DAVID BRIN**, a prolific speculative author, spoke about "Gaia, Freedom, and Human Nature." His concept of information in a rapidly shrinking world is wonderfully developed in his most recent success, the very popular book, *Earth.*

- **BRUCE STERLING** is one of the founders of the highly influential "cyberpunk" movement. His books include the internationally bestselling collection of cyberpunk stories, *Mirrorshades*. "Free as Air, Free as Water, Free as Knowledge" addresses crucial information technology issues for all of us.

Simply put, there are significant ethical, societal, and management issues that face us as technology is more and more incorporated into our lives. Values can get lost in the technology, but the love of humanity and the love of technology are not by nature mutually exclusive. The purpose of the 1992 LITA President's Program was to awaken the audience and now you, the reader, to possibilities and to call to you to join us in accepting responsibility for that future. This publication contains the speakers' presentations and background essays in support of their vision. Hopefully, it will help your vision to grow. We want you be empowered by becoming informed.

DON'T STOP READING! This book is definitely not one long boring lecture. If you decide to skip anything, bypass this introduction. On the pages that follow, you will find fiction, brilliant insights, wild (but plausible) thoughts, and stunning presentations. Obfuscation and heavy technological presentations were forbidden concepts for these authors. They were charged to deliver inspired writing and they did.

Why do we care so much about the quality of the writing? Perhaps it's time to tell you about the genesis of the LITA Imagineering Interest Group.

The Imagineers

Paul Peters brought Milton Wolf, Charles Bailey, and me together a few years ago with the goal of starting a new interest group in LITA, the

Imagineering Interest Group. The name was borrowed from Walt Disney Studios and is very simply a combination of *imagination* and *engineering*. Paul's premise was that imagination and mystery are important things for technologists (library or otherwise) to cultivate at this time in world history. Now, if you want the real truth, I have to admit that we had public agendas, private agendas, and even different agendas for each of us. But we had one thing in common: each of us has a lifelong love of speculative writing.

So that's the first, but not necessarily public, agenda. The group came together because of our love of good ideas, but we also carried an implicit suspicion about someone who purports to have one of those good ideas but can't seem to get it written down in a manner that a normal person can understand. You see, if you can't *write* clearly, then it sure seems like you probably can't *think* clearly either. This defined our territory: "Writers" with a capital "W." No hacks need apply. Needless to say, when Milton and I began work on this publication we realized that we had no choice but to create something that would measure up to our standards. The result is in the pages that follow. We tried hard, and I hope you will think we have succeeded.

How about an official agenda? On paper, the goal of the Imagineering Interest Group is "to promote imaginative forecasting and planning for future information systems and technologies by the examination and analysis of science fiction themes and works." I've heard Paul refer to this as non-linear strategic planning. I've also heard it said that forecasting is rhetoric for thinking about the present. Does it work? I'd say so. My everyday job is to provide leadership for information technology. Whenever I start us on a significant new direction, the inevitable question from my boss has been, "What are you reading *now*?" The embarrassing part is that I usually *have* been reading something really stimulating ... almost always recommended by Paul, Milton, or Charles. The *Books About the Future* appendix is solely composed of those titles.

Yes, we do love good authors. This has lead us to a simple but satisfying format for meetings. Twice a year, at ALA Annual and Midwinter Conferences, we arrange for one of our favorite authors to drop by for an hour to visit. It's nothing formal. We're just an interest group. The authors share their visionary ideas, and the group asks questions. To date, we've been treated to Hal Clement, Fred Pohl, Elizabeth Anne Hull, Pat Cadigan, and Elizabeth Moon. (Too bad for you if you missed the writing talent that was around after this program!) The agenda is simple: provide the audience with an opportunity for a little enlightenment.

How about another agenda? We rather presumptuously are out to co-opt the authors. LITA members know a lot about information technology and are positioned to have valuable insights into emerging issues. The catch is that we write for and communicate with each other. A large readership for any of us is usually five or maybe ten thousand people. A science fiction author reaches two hundred thousand readers with a single printing of one book. Not only that, by definition they write well and can persuade readers to embrace their thinking. If we can convey possibilities and problems about technology and about the management of information to these authors, they can incorporate that knowledge into their work. We can use their skills and their distribution to reach a much bigger audience!

The Words on the Following Pages

The writers in this publication were charged to provide background for the audience and future readers. The emphasis has been on concepts and terms of reference that define visions of the future and issues and concerns that are presented by progress toward those visions.

A significant goal has been to reach a group that would not even consider reading speculative writing, be it fiction or non-fiction. This is an important opportunity to share values and insights, and we have been careful to avoid scaring away anyone who might be intimidated by advanced technology or who might profess lack of interest in the future or who would never read "pulp science fiction." However, as I indicated above, we did not prepare bland, watered down essays. Quite the contrary. The writers were indeed inspired.

Information Technology offers the potential for improved quality of life. Will that improvement be found simply in improved education and health care, or does it mean replacing humanity with robots? Before rejecting that thought as an impossibility, read on. Try Hans Moravec, *Slouch Toward the Future* with Milton Wolf, and take a peek at Howard Davidson's *Clear Vision*.

Information Technology offers the potential for transcendence. This is an important and basic human value that could become available for the masses instead of the elite few. William Lidwell and Kim Trull share a beautiful vision in their *Transreal Experience*, and David Porush pushes the boundaries when he finds *Transcendence at the Interface*.

Information Technology is having a profound influence on politics and the world order. The failure of the recent USSR coup is perhaps due more than anything else to the inability to shut down communications and computing technology. The context for this quote varies, but one aspect definitely applies here: "Information wants to be free." Read David Brin's remarks and contemplate Kathy Fladland's appraisal of his book *Earth* and how the Internet has already become an entity.

Information Technology can set information free, but it also forces us to be responsible as individuals. A simple communication that reaches millions instantly can have profound implications. Sonia Lyris gives us rules for living in *Crime and Punishment in Cyberspace*, and Steve Cisler tells about the *Canary on the Computer*.

I've slighted the other authors by not listing them here, but I want you to read them and not me. Read on!

Your charge as a reader is to trust us. If the writing or the topic in a particular article doesn't draw you in, set it aside and try another one. There are some real treats in these pages.

Acknowledgement

Special thanks are due to Jerry Kline and Steve Silberstein from Innovative Interfaces, Inc. who wrote the check to pay for the paper and printing for the version that was distributed to the audience at the program. Be sure to thank the authors for their creative vision, but don't forget to thank Jerry and Steve for their help with the project, too.

About The Editors

R. Bruce Miller thought he was a rare book librarian but wandered into library technical services and systems work and got lost along the way. He's been busy in LITA for years and currently is a member of the Board of Directors. Trusting some old friends, he walked wide eyed into the LITA Imagineering Interest Group and met Milton. That led to this collaboration: another publication that doesn't quite typify "regular" library literature to go along with his other writings about Russian computer keyboards, VDT health issues, and the romanization of Chinese. Library life began at the Humanities Research Center at the University of Texas at Austin and has led to his current position as head of technical services and systems at the University of California, San Diego. Internet: rbmiller@ucsd.edu

Milton T. Wolf has worked at Pennsylvania State University, University of North Carolina—Chapel Hill, Wright State University, and the

University of Nevada, Reno. He has over 60 publications in different fields, was the founding editor of *Technicalities*, and has written for *Locus*, *Library Journal*, and *The New Encyclopedia of Science Fiction*. Currently he is at work on a book with the working title of *Future Sex*. He is Assistant University Librarian for Collection Development at the University of Nevada, Reno. He has taught classes in science fiction, global information dissemination, research and bibliography, handball, back-country skiing, and acquisition of library materials. When not writing, reading, or traveling, he enjoys the great outdoors with his faithful companion Tonka-Sierra (part wolf, of course). Internet: sfwolf@unssun.unr.edu

...Without Mind Food We Can't...

Below is an exact transcription of a letter I recently received. I have every reason to believe that the request is legitimate. I also believe that it is deeply relevant to the content of this book you have in hand. Regardless, even if the request turns out to be fradulent, it still seems worthwhile to respond because sooner or later any books that are sent will be read by someone who may not otherwise have had access to them.—*R. Bruce Miller*

Zoryany Shlyah SF club
c/o Boris Sidyuk
Poste Restante
General P.O.
Kiev 252001
Ukraine
December 12, 1991

Dear sir or madam,

We are a SF club called Zoryany Shlyah of Kiev, the capital of Ukraine (former Soviet republic, now an independent country). We are the only one in the former USSR who have the section of English-readings in the club. We even issue our English-language publication called *CHERNOBYLIZA-TION* well-known throughout the world.

As you probably know the situation in the former Soviet empire is going on very hard. The people here have lots of problems to survive and live. It is also hard time for SF community in this country, a part thereof we are.

We read SF books, we do love to read ones, to study SF&F in general, to enjoy this wonderful world. But know we almost have not got books for reading. It's a whole problem for us, more one than, for example, to find food. We can go hungry, but without mind food we can't.

As far as we know your library takes off, from time to time, old SF&F books and sells them for lowest prices. We do need them, but we have no cents (I do not mention dollars) to buy even a single of. You do not need soviet wooden dried Roubles. It seems no way out. But maybe we and you can exchange. You can send us your taken-off books. And we can send you

7

new SF&F books published here in russian and ukrainian, both by local authors and translated from English. Please, let us know what you think of it.

Looking forward to hearing from you soon.

On behalf of the club,

Yours faithfully,

Boris Sidyuk, chairman

The Speakers

Introduction to the 1992 LITA President's Program

Milton T. Wolf

Science fiction's main goal is generally not to predict the future but to extrapolate on the present; however, it is almost a media cliche anymore to hear that science fiction has just turned into fact again. We have gone to the moon, we do have robots, and, yes, we are rapidly becoming cyborgs as we attach ourselves to a panoply of robotic gadgets: artificial hearts, livers, limbs, and a host of biosensors. The TV character who starred in *The Six Million Dollar Man* was essentially a cyborg. Although most of us are the couple hundred dollar model, it won't be long (especially given the proclivities of the American medical profession) before many of us will become progressively more **expensive** cyborgs.

Even though science fiction spent its adolescence in the ghetto of the pulp magazines, shunned by the arbiters of highbrow taste, it, not unlike the field of librarianship, came to a quick maturity as the Information Age unceremoniously catapulted both professions front and center onto the world stage of an increasingly New Order. Science fiction has intersected mainstream culture and has become a "mode of awareness," a significant way of conceptualizing our cultural condition.

Like librarianship, science fiction finds itself in a privileged position. It, more than any other genre, mirrors and engages the technological culture which is coming to pervade every aspect of human society. Today we are honored to have with us three of the most outstanding representatives of this cultural dialectic, one that will take us to the edge of technology—and hopefully to freedom.

Hans Moravec is the world's foremost mobile roboticist. He has suggested that we are disappearing into our machines. "We are," he has

11

stated, "very near the time when virtually no essential human function, physical or mental, will lack an artificial counterpart." Since the brain is an extraordinary processor of information, we may be able to "download" it into robotic bodies. Immortality, maybe; stupid robots, guaranteed. Imagine the power of gods before us. Hans has explored that territory and will share with us his adventures.

Bruce Sterling has been called the Robin Hood of the Data Forest. Often speaking for the Unspeakable, he has sounded the call about exploitation, commodification, and downright treachery on the Electronic Frontier. Providing much of the philosophical underpinnings of the "cyberpunk movement," Bruce is an expert on the denizens of cyberspace, that computer-generated reality that opens ever further the human imagination—for good or ill. When law only protects the powerful, the vested interests, the franchised wealthy, some champion of necessity is coughed up from the streets to stir the rag-tag throng into less than passive acceptance.

David Brin has synthesized an enormous amount of fact and knowledge from numerous fields, rolled it into a ball about the size of the earth, and put many of our brains into a conceptual spin. David has called science fiction writers "the little literary cabal who form the R&D division of the Department of Myths and Legends of the new culture. We are scouts, the ones who explore the edges, who point out dangers that may lurk, not just on the horizon but perhaps some distance beyond it. We warn of possible mistakes and create chilling scenarios to make them mythically believable. And in so doing, we hope to *prevent* them from coming true." He also has the vision of an optimist who thinks we are capable of more wisdom than folly...maybe a bit more hope than despair.

Hans Moravec

...original thinker, paradigm changer, visionary, philosopher

...worldrenownedroboticist
  (a new word apparently made up just to describe Moravec...
  at least it always seems to be used in conjunction with his name)

...author of *Mind Children: The Future of Robot and Human Intelligence*

...*The Age of Mind* (1993—hopefully) will push the ideas further.

> The concept and research originally came out of the Moravec-Minsky immortality quest. Those pioneers of artificial intelligence, Hans Moravec at Carnegie-Mellon and Marvin Minsky at MIT, believed an individual brain could be entirely imported into a computer program and supercopied. The human body would become superfluous. When the body died, the program could be housed in a robotic body, and the individual's consciousness could live forever.
>
> Immortality.
> > Lisa Mason, *Arachne* (New York: Morrow, 1990), 70-71.

*Thinking Robots
An Aware Internet
and
Cyberpunk Librarians*

Pigs in Cyberspace

Hans Moravec

Exploration and colonization of the universe awaits, but earth-adapted biological humans are ill-equipped to respond to the challenge. Machines have gone farther and seen more, limited though they presently are by insect-like behavioral inflexibility. As they become smarter over the coming decades, space will be theirs. Organizations of robots of ever increasing intelligence and sensory and motor ability will expand and transform what they occupy, working with matter, space, and time. As they grow, a smaller and smaller fraction of their territory will be undeveloped frontier. Competitive success will depend more and more on using already available matter and space in ever more refined and useful forms. The process, analogous to the miniaturization that makes today's computers a trillion times more powerful than the mechanical calculators of the past, will gradually transform all activity from grossly physical homesteading of raw nature, to minimum-energy quantum transactions of computation. The final frontier will be urbanized, ultimately into an arena where every bit of activity is meaningful computation: the inhabited portion of the universe will be transformed into a cyberspace.

Because it will use resources more efficiently, a mature cyberspace of the distant future will be effectively *much* bigger than the present physical universe. While only an infinitesimal fraction of existing matter and space is doing interesting work, in a well developed cyberspace every bit will be part of a relevant computation or will be storing a useful datum. Over time, more compact and faster ways of using space and matter will be invented and used to restructure the cyberspace, effectively increasing the amount of computational spacetime per unit of physical spacetime.

Computational speedups will affect the subjective experience of entities in the cyberspace in a paradoxical way. At first glimpse, there is no subjective effect, because everything, inside and outside the individual, speeds up equally. But, more subtly, speedup produces an expansion of the cyber universe, because, as thought accelerates, more *subjective* time passes during the fixed (probably lightspeed) *physical* transit time of a message between a given pair of locations—so those fixed locations seem to grow farther apart. Also, as information storage is made continually more efficient through both denser utilization of matter and more efficient encodings, there will be increasingly more cyber-stuff between any two points. The effect may somewhat resemble the continuous-creation process in the old steady-state theory of the physical universe of Hoyle, Bondi, and Gold, where hydrogen atoms appear just fast enough throughout the expanding cosmos to maintain a constant density.

A quantum-mechanical entropy calculation by Bekenstein suggests that the ultimate amount of information that can be stored given the mass and volume of a hydrogen atom is about a megabyte. But let's be conservative and imagine that at some point in the future only "conventional" physics is in play, but every few atoms stores a useful bit. There are about 10^{56} atoms in the solar system. I estimate that a human brain-equivalent can be encoded in less than 10^{15} bits. If a body and surrounding environment take a thousand times more storage in addition, a human, with immediate environment, might consume 10^{18} bits. An AI with equivalent intelligence could probably get by with less, since it does without the body-simulation "life support" needed to keep a body-oriented human mind sane. So a city of a million human-scale inhabitants might be efficiently stored in 10^{24} bits. If the atoms of the solar system were cleverly rearranged so every 100 could represent a bit, then a single solar system could hold 10^{30} cities—far more than the number (10^{22}) of stars in the *visible universe*! Multiply that by 10^{11} stars in a galaxy, and one gets 10^{41} cities per galaxy. The visible universe, with 10^{11} galaxies, would then have room for 10^{52} cities—except that by the time intelligence has expanded that far, more efficient ways of using spacetime and encoding data would surely have been discovered, increasing the number much further.

Mind without Body?

Start with the concepts of telepresence and virtual reality. You wear a harness that, with optical, acoustical, mechanical, and chemical devices controls all that you sense and measures all of your actions. Its machinery presents pictures to your eyes, sounds to your ears, pressures and temperatures to your skin, forces to your muscles, and even smells and tastes for the remaining senses. Telepresence results when the inputs and outputs of this harness connect to a distant machine that looks like a humanoid robot. The images from the robot's two camera eyes appear on your "eyeglass" viewscreens, and you hear through its ears, feel through its skin, and smell through its chemical sensors. When you move your head or body, the robot moves in exact synchrony. When you reach for an object seen in the viewscreens, the robot reaches for the object, and when it makes contact, your muscles and skin feel the resulting weight, shape, texture, and temperature. For most practical purposes you inhabit the robot's body—your sense of consciousness has migrated to the robot's location, in a true "out of body" experience.

Virtual reality retains the harness but replaces the remote robot with a computer simulation of a body and its surroundings. When connected to a virtual reality, the location you seem to inhabit does not exist in the usual physical sense, rather you are in a kind of computer-generated dream. If the computer has access to data from the outside world, the simulation may contain some "real" items, for instance representations of other people connected via their own harnesses, or even views of the outside world, perhaps through simulated windows.

One might imagine a hybrid system where a virtual "central station" is surrounded by portals that open on to views of multiple real locations. While in the station one inhabits a simulated body, but when one steps through a portal, the harness link is seamlessly switched from the simulation to a telepresence robot waiting at that location.

The technical challenges limit the availability, "fidelity," and affordability of telepresence and virtual reality systems today—in fact, they exist only in a few highly experimental demonstrations. But progress is being made, and it's possible to anticipate a time, a few decades hence, when people spend more time in remote and virtual realities than in their immediate surroundings, just as today most of us spend more time in artificial indoor surroundings than in the great outdoors. The remote bodies we will inhabit can be stronger, faster and have better senses than our "home" body. In fact, as our home body ages and weakens, we might compensate by turning up some kind of "volume control." Eventually, we might wish to bypass our atrophied muscles and dimmed senses altogether, if neurobiology learns enough to connect our sensory and motor nerves directly to electronic interfaces. Then all the harness hardware could be discarded as obsolete, along with our sense organs and muscles, and indeed most of our body. There would be no "home" experiences to return to, but our remote and virtual existence would be better than ever.

The picture is that we are now a "brain in a vat," sustained by life-support machinery, and connected by wonderful electronic links, at will, to a series of "rented" artificial bodies at remote locations, or to simulated bodies in artificial realities. But the brain is a biological machine not designed to function forever, even in an optimal physical environment. As it begins to malfunction, might we not choose to use the same advanced neurological electronics that make possible our links to the external world, to replace the gray matter as it begins to fail? Bit by bit our brain is replaced by electronic equivalents, which work at least as well, leaving our personality and thoughts clearer than ever. Eventually everything has been replaced by manufactured parts. No vestige of our original body remains, but our thoughts and awareness continue. We will call this process, and other approaches with the same end result, the *downloading* of a human mind into a machine. After downloading, our personality is a pattern impressed on electronic hardware, and we may then find ways to move our minds to other similar hardware, just as a computer program and its data can be copied from processor to processor. So not only can our sense of awareness shift from place to place at the speed of communication, but the very components of our minds may ride on the same data channels. We might find ourselves distributed over many locations, one piece of our mind here, another piece there, and our sense of awareness at yet another place. Time becomes more flexible—when our mind resides in very fast hardware, one second of real time may provide a subjective year of thinking time, while a thousand years of real time spent on a passive storage medium may seem like no time at all. Can we then consider ourselves to be a mind without a body? Not quite.

A human totally deprived of bodily senses does not do well. After twelve hours in a sensory deprivation tank (where one floats in a body-temperature saline solution that produces almost no skin sensation, in total darkness and silence, with taste and smell and the sensations of breathing minimized) a subject will begin to hallucinate, as the mind, somewhat like a television tuned to a nonexistent channel, turns up the amplification, desperately looking for a signal, becoming ever less discriminating in the theories it offers to make sense of the random sensory hiss it receives. Even the most extreme telepresence and virtual reality scenarios we have presented avoid complete bodilessness by always providing the mind with a consistent sensory (and motor) image, obtained from an actual remote robot body, or from a computer simulation. In those scenarios, a person may sometimes exist without a physical body but never without the illusion of having one.

But in our computers there are already many entities that resemble truly bodiless minds. A typical computer chess program knows nothing about physical chess pieces or chessboards, or about the staring eyes of its opponent, or the bright lights of a tournament. Nor does it work with an internal simulation of those physical attributes. It reasons instead with a very efficient and compact mathematical representation of chess positions and moves. For the benefit of human players this internal representation is sometimes translated to a recognizable graphic on a computer screen, but such images mean nothing to the program that actually chooses the chess moves. For all practical purposes, the chess program's thoughts and sensations—its consciousness—is pure chess, with no taint of the physical, or any other, world. Much more than a human mind with a simulated body stored in a computer, a chess program is a mind without a body.

So now, imagine a future world where programs that do chess, mathematics, physics, engineering, art, business, or whatever, have grown up to become at least as clever as the human mind. Imagine also that most of the human universe has been converted to a computer network—a cyberspace —where such programs live, side by side with downloaded human minds and accompanying simulated human bodies. Suppose that all these entities make their living in something of a free market way, trading the products of their labor for the essentials of life in this world—memory space and computing cycles. Some entities do the equivalent of manual work, converting undeveloped parts of the universe into cyberspace or improving the performance of existing patches, thus creating new wealth. Others act as banks, storing and redistributing resources, buying and selling computing space, time, and information. Some we might class as artists, creating structures that don't obviously result in physical resources, but which, for idiosyncratic reasons, are deemed valuable by some customers and are traded at prices that fluctuate for subjective reasons. Some entities in the cyberspace will fail to produce enough value to support their requirements for existence—these eventually shrink and disappear, or merge with other ventures. Others will succeed and grow. The closest present day parallel is the growth, evolution, fragmentation, and consolidation of corporations, whose options are shaped primarily by their economic performance.

A human would likely fare poorly in such a cyberspace. Unlike the streamlined artificial intelligences that zip about, making discoveries and deals, reconfiguring themselves to efficiently handle the data that constitutes their interactions, a human mind would lumber about in a massively inappropriate body simulation, analogous to someone in a deep diving suit plodding along among a troupe of acrobatic dolphins. Every interaction with the data world would first have to be analogized as some recognizable quasi-physical entity: other programs might be presented as animals, plants, or demons, data items such as books or treasure chests, accounting entities as coins or gold. Maintaining such fictions increases the cost of doing business, as odes operating the mind machinery that reduces the physical simulations into mental abstractions in the downloaded human mind. Though a few humans may find a niche exploiting their baroque construction to produce human flavored art, more may feel a great economic incentive to streamline their interface to the cyberspace.

The streamlining could begin with the elimination of the body simulation along with the portions of the downloaded mind dedicated to interpreting sense-data. These would be replaced with simpler integrated programs that produced approximately the same net effect in one's consciousness. One would still view the cyber world in terms of location, color, smell, faces, and so on, but only those details we actually notice would be represented. We would still be at a disadvantage compared with the true artificial intelligences, who interact with the cyberspace in ways optimized for their tasks. We might then be tempted to replace some of our innermost mental processes with more cyberspace-appropriate programs purchased from the AIs, and so, bit by bit, transform ourselves into something much like them. Ultimately our thinking procedures could be totally liberated from any traces of our original body, indeed of any body. But the bodiless mind that results, wonderful though it may be in its clarity of thought and breadth of understanding, could in no sense be considered any longer human.

So, in one way or another, the immensities of cyberspace will be teeming with very unhuman disembodied superminds, engaged in affairs of the future that are to human concerns as ours are to bacteria. But, once in a long while, humans do think of bacteria, even particular bacteria seen in particular microscopes. Similarly, a cyberbeing may occasionally bring to mind a human event of the distant past. If a sufficiently powerful mind makes a sufficiently large effort, such recall could occur with great detail—call it high fidelity. With enough fidelity, the situation of a remembered person, along with all the minutiae of her body, her thoughts, and her feelings would be perfectly recreated in a kind of mental simulation: a cyberspace within a cyberspace where the person would be as alive there as anywhere. Sometimes the recall might be historically accurate, in other circumstances it could be artificially enhanced: it depends on the circumstances of the cybermind. An evolving cyberspace becomes effectively ever more capacious and long lasting and so can support ever more minds of ever greater power. If these minds spend only an infinitesimal fraction of their energy contemplating the human past, their sheer power should ensure that eventually our entire history is replayed many times, in many places, and in many variations. The very moment we are now experiencing may actually be (almost certainly is) such a distributed mental event and most likely is a complete fabrication that never happened physically. Alas, there is no way to sort it out from our perspective: we can only wallow in the scenery.

Bruce Sterling

...author, editor, journalist, critic, cyberpunk role model

...science fiction novels, stories, and editorial work abound, the best known are:
Involution Ocean (1977)
The Artificial Kid (1980)
Schismatrix (1985)
Mirrorshades: The Cyberpunk Anthology (1986)
Islands in the Net (1988)
Crystal Express (1990)
The Difference Engine (1990, with William Gibson)

...*The Hacker Crackdown* (nonfiction) about computer crime and civil liberties issues is on its way.

They created an artificial reality: telespace.

Individual mental access via telelink into a collective program. Theoreticians suggested that the technology resembled the twentieth-century notion of the collective unconscious. Never widely understood or accepted, the great analyst Carl Jung defined the collective unconscious as the matrix of the human mind and its inventions. A body of psychic energy comprised of magical, symbolical, mythical, historical, and psychological referents. Jung proposed that this matrix existed independently of the human individual. That the matrix was inherited, perpetually maintained, and manifested in ways scarcely realized by each individual, in his or her life, through the ages of humanity.

Lisa Mason, Arachne (New York: Morrow, 1990), 71.

Thinking Robots
An Aware Internet
and
Cyberpunk Librarians

Free As Air, Free As Water, Free As Knowledge

Bruce Sterling

Hi, everybody. Well, this is the Library and Information Technology Association, so I guess I ought to be talking about libraries, or information, or technology, or at least association. I'm gonna give it a shot, but I want to try this from an unusual perspective. I want to start by talking about money.

You wouldn't guess it sometimes to hear some people talk, but we don't live in a technocratic information society. We live in a highly advanced capitalist society. People talk about the power and glory of specialized knowledge and technical expertise. Knowledge is power—but if so, why aren't knowledgeable people in power? It's true there's a Library OF Congress. But how many librarians are there IN Congress?

The nature of our society strongly affects the nature of our technology. It doesn't absolutely *determine* it; a lot of our technology is sheer accident, serendipity, the way the cards happened to fall, who got the lucky breaks, and, of course, the occasional eruption of *genius*, which tends to be positively unpredictable by its nature. But as a society we don't develop technologies to their ultimate ends. Only engineers are interested in that kind of technical sweetness, and engineers generally have their paychecks signed by CEOs and stockholders. We don't pursue ultimate technologies. Our technologies are actually designed and produced to optimize the financial return on investment. There's a big difference.

Of course there are many elements of our lives that exist outside the money economy. There's a lot going on in our lives that's not-for-profit that can't be denominated in dollars. "The best things in life are free," the old saying goes. Nice old saying. Gets a little older-sounding every day. Sounds about as old and mossy as the wedding vow "for richer or poorer," which in a modern environment is pretty likely to be for-richer-or-poorer modulo our prenuptial agreement. Commercialization. Commodification, a favorite buzzword of mine. It's a very powerful phenomenon. It seems to me to be getting more powerful year by year.

Academia, libraries, cultural institutions are under protracted commercial siege. This is MacNeil Lehrer News Hour, brought to you by publicly supported television and, incidentally, AT&T. Welcome students to Large Northeastern University, brought to you by Pepsi-Cola, official drink of Large Northeastern. Ye shall know the truth, and the truth shall make ye employable. Hi, I'm the head of the microbiology department here at Large Northeastern. I'm also on the board of directors of TransGenic Corporation. The Chancellor says it's ok because a cut of the patent money goes to Large Northeastern.

Welcome to the Library of Congress. Jolt Cola is the official drink of the Library of Congress. This is our distributed electronic data network, brought to you by Prodigy Services, a joint venture of IBM and Sears. You'll notice the banner of bright-red ads that spools by your eyeballs while you're trying to access the electronic full-text of William Wordsworth. Try to pay no attention to that. Incidentally, there's a Hypertext link here where you can order our Wordsworth T-shirt and have it billed to your credit card. Did I mention that the Library of Congress is now also a bank? Hey, data is data! Digits are digits! Every pixel in cyberspace is a potential sales opportunity. Be sure to visit our library coffee-bar, too. You can rent videos here if you want. We do souvenir umbrellas, ashtrays, earrings, fridge magnets, the works. We librarians are doing what we can to survive this economically difficult period. After all, the library is a regrettably old-fashioned institution which has not been honed into fighting trim by exposure to healthy market competition. Until now, that is!

The American library system was invented in a different cultural climate. This is how it happened. You're Benjamin Franklin, a printer by trade and your average universal genius, and it's the Year of Our Lord 1731. You have this freewheeling debating club called the Junto, and you decide you're going to pool your books and charge everybody a very small fee to join in and read them. There's about fifty of you. You're not big people, in the Junto. You're not aristocrats or well-born people or even philanthropists. You're mostly apprentices and young people who work with their hands. If you were rich, you wouldn't be so anxious to pool your information in the first place. So you put all your leatherbound books into the old Philadelphia clubhouse, and you charge people forty shillings to join and ten shillings dues per annum.

Now forget 1731. It's 1991. Forget the leatherbound books. You start swapping floppy disks and using a bulletin board system. Public spirited? A benefit to society? Democratic institution, knowledge is power, power to the people? Maybe ... or maybe you're an idealistic nut, Mr. Franklin. Not only that, but you're menacing our commercial interests! What about our trade secrets, Mr. Franklin? Our trademarks, copyrights, and patents. Our intellectual property rights. Our look-and-feel. Our patented algorithms. Our national security clearances. Our export licenses. Our FBI surveillance policy. Don't copy that floppy, Mr. Franklin! And you're telling me you want us to pay *taxes* to support your suspicious activities? Hey, if there's a real need here, the market will meet it, Mr. Franklin. I really think this "library" idea of yours something better left to the private sector, Mr. Franklin. No author could possibly want his books read for free, sir. Are you trying to starve the creative artist?

Let's get real, Mr. Franklin. You know what's real, Mr. Franklin? Money is real. You seem to be under the misapprehension that information should be free and that enabling people to learn and follow their own interests will benefit society as a whole. Well, we no longer believe in society as a whole. We believe in the *economy* as a whole—a black hole! Why should you be able to think things, and even learn things, without paying somebody for that privilege? Let's get to brass tacks, the bottom line. Money. Money is reality. You see this printed dollar bill? It's far more real than topsoil or oxygen or the ozone layer or sunlight. You may say that what we call reality is just a piece of paper with some symbols on it, but that's sacrilege! This is the Almighty Dollar. Most of the dollars we worship are actually stored in cyberspace. Dollars are just digital ones and zeros in a network of computers, but that doesn't mean they're only virtual reality and basically one big fantasy. No, dollars are utterly and entirely real, far more real than anything as vague as the public interest. If you're not a commodity, you don't exist!

Can you believe that Melvil Dewey once said, "free as air, free as water, free as knowledge?" Free as knowledge? Let's get real, this is the modern world—air and water no longer come cheap! Hey, you want breathable air, you better pay your air conditioner's power-bill, pal. Free as water? Man, if you've got sense you buy the bottled variety or pay for an ionic filter on your tap. And free as knowledge? Well, we don't know what "knowledge" is, but we can get you plenty of *data*, and as soon as we can figure out how to download it straight into student skulls, we can put all the teachers into the breadline and librarians as well.

Ladies and gentlemen, there's a basic problem with showing Mr. Franklin the door. The problem is that Mr. Franklin was right, and Mr. Franklin is *still* right. Information is not something you can successfully peddle like Coca-Cola. If it were a genuine commodity, then information would cost nothing when you had a glut of it. God knows we've got enough data! We're drowning in data. Nevertheless we're only gonna make more. Money just does not map the world of information at all well. How much is the Bible worth? You can get a Bible in any hotel room. They're worthless as commodities but not valueless to mankind. Money and value are not identical.

What's information *really* about? It seems to me there's something direly wrong with the *Information Economy*. It's not about data, it's about attention. In a few years you may be able to carry the Library of Congress in your hip pocket. So? You're never gonna read the Library of Congress. You'll die long before you access one tenth of one percent of it. What's important—*increasingly important*—is the process by which you figure out what to look at. This is the beginning of the real and true economics of information—not who owns the books, who prints the books, who has the holdings. The crux today is *access*, not holdings. And not even *access* itself but the signposts that tell you *what* to access—what to pay attention to. In the Information Economy *everything* is plentiful—except attention.

That's why the spin doctor is the creature who increasingly rules the information universe. *Spin doctors* rule our attention. Never mind that man behind the curtain. No, no! Look at my hand! I can make a candidate disappear. Watch me pull a President out of a hat. Look! I can make these homeless people disappear in a haze of media noise. Nothing up my sleeve. Presto! The facts don't matter if he can successfully direct our *attention*. Spin doctors are like evil anti-librarians; they're the Dark Side of the Force.

Librarians used to be book-pullers. Book-pullers. I kind of like the humble, workaday sound of that. I like it kind of better than I like the sound of "information retrieval expert," though that's clearly where librarians are headed. Might be the right way to head. That's where the power seems to be. Though I wonder exactly what will be retrieved and what will be allowed to quietly mummify in the deepest darkest deserts of the dustiest hard-disks.

I like libraries and librarians, I owe my career to libraries and librarians. I respect Mr. Franklin. I hate seeing books turned into a commodity and seeing access to books turned into a commodity. I do like bookstores, too, and, of course, I earn my living by them, but I worry about them more and more. I don't like chainstores, and I don't like chain distributors. We already have twelve human beings in the US who buy all the science fiction books for the twelve major American distributors. They're the information filters and the attention filters, and their criterion is the bottom line, and the bottom line is bogus and a fraud. I don't like megapublishers either. Modern publishing is owned by far too few people. They're the people who own the means of production, and worse yet, they own far too much of the means of attention. They determine what we get to pay attention to.

Of course, there are other ways, other methods, of delimiting people s attention besides merely commercial ones. Like aesthetic and cultural means of limiting attention. Librarians used to be very big on this kind of public spirited filtering. Conceivably, librarians could get this way again with another turn of the cultural wheel. Librarians could become very correct. Holdings must be thinned, and even in electronic media the good old *delete* key is never far from hand. Try reading what librarians used to say a hundred years ago. Your ancestral librarians were really upset about popular novels. They carried on about novels in a tone of voice which would sound very familiar to Dan Quayle. Here's a gentleman named Dr. Isaac Ray in the 1870's. I quote him: "The specific doctrine I would inculcate is, that the excessive indulgence in novel-reading, which is a characteristic of our times, is chargeable with many of the mental irregularities that prevail upon us to a degree unknown at any former period."

Here's the superintendent of education for the State of Michigan in 1869. "The state swarms with peddlers of the sensational novels of all ages, tales of piracy, murders, and love intrigues—the yellow-covered literature of the world." Librarian James Angell in 1904: "I think it must be confessed that a great deal of the fiction which is deluging the market is the veriest trash, or worse than trash. Much of it is positively bad in its influence. It awakens morbid passions. It deals in the most exaggerated representations of life. It is vicious in style."

These worthies are talking about the authors who corrupt the values of youth, authors who write about crime and lowlife, authors who drive people nuts, authors who themselves are degraded and untrustworthy and quite possibly insane. I think I know who they are talking about. Basically they're talking about **me**.

Here's the President of the United States speaking at a library in 1890. "The boy who greedily devours the vicious tales of imaginary daring and blood-curdling adventure, which in these days are far too accessible, will have his brain filled with notions of life and standards of manliness which, if they do not make him a menace to peace and good order, will certainly not make him a useful member of society." Grover Cleveland hit the nail on the head. I feel very strongly, I feel instinctively, I feel passionately that I am one of those nails. Not only did I start out in libraries as that greedy devouring boy, but thanks to mindwarping science fictional yellow-covered literature, I have become a menace to Grover Cleveland's idea of peace and good order.

Far too accessible, eh, Mr President? Too much access. By all means let's not provide our electronic networks with *too much access*. That might get dangerous. The networks might rot people's minds and corrupt their family values. They might create bad taste. Do you think this electrical network thing is a new social problem? Think again. Listen to prominent litterateur James Russell Lowell speaking in 1885. "We diligently inform ourselves, and cover the continent with speaking wires... we are getting buried alive under this avalanche of earthly impertinences... we... are willing to become mere sponges saturated from the stagnant goosepond of village gossip."

The stagnant goosepond of the *global* village. Marshall McLuhan's stagnant goosepond. Who are the geese in the stagnant pond? Whoever they are, I'm one of them. You'll find me with the pulp magazines and the bloodcurdling comics and the yellow-covered works of imaginary daring. In the future you'll find me or my successors in the electronic pulps. In the electronic zines, in the fanzines, in the digital genres, the digital underground. In whatever medium it is that really bugs Grover Cleveland. He can't make up his mind whether I'm the scum from the gutter or the "cultural elite"—but in either case he doesn't like me.

He doesn't like cyberpunks. That's not big news to you people I'm sure. But he's not going to like cyberpunk librarians either. I hope you won't deceive yourselves on that score.

Weird ideas are tolerable as long as they remain weird ideas. Once they start actually challenging the world, there's smoke in the air and blood on the floor. You cybernetic LITA guys are marching toward blood on the floor. It's cultural struggle, political struggle, legal struggle. Extending the public right-to-know into cyberspace will be a mighty battle. It's an old war, a war librarians are used to, and I honor you for the free-expression battles you have won in the past. But the terrain of cyberspace is new terrain. I think that ground will have to be won all over again, megabyte by megabyte.

You've heard some weird ideas today. That's what we're here for—weird ideas. I like reading Hans Moravec. I respect him, and I pay close attention to what he says. When he was talking here, I was taking notes. He's a true fount of weird ideas, and in my opinion he's a credit to the basic values of the American republic. I think he even makes a certain amount of sense, technically and rationally, if not politically and socially.

But then again, I don't think the Ayatollahs have read *Mind Children* yet. If they had, they would recognize it as complete and utter blasphemy, far worse than Salman Rushdie's *Satanic Verses*. If Hans actually got around to creating a digital afterlife right here on Earth, I'm pretty sure the Moslem fundamentalists would try to have him killed. They'd surely consider this their solemn moral duty. And they probably wouldn't be the first in line, either. A lot of people have seen the science fiction film, *Terminator 2*. They might figure our friend here as the future Architect of Skynet. He wants to make the human race obsolete and let robots rule. Doesn't that mean it'd be a lot more convenient to kill him right now?

Of course we're not going to kill Hans now. I mean not until he gets his own satellite channel and starts his own religious movement. Not till he starts building a posthuman brain in a box. When his technology moves from the rhetorical to the commercial and *Mind Children* becomes *Mind Children*™ and they're manufactured by Apple and Toshiba and retailed to adventurous aging yuppies. Fifty years to the singularity? Fifty years to the complete transformation of the human condition? Maybe. Maybe it's just five years till the day the Secret Service raids the basement at MIT and removes all of Hans' equipment. As for criminal charges, well, they'll think of something. Maybe they can nail him on an FDA rap.

I do kind of believe in the singularity though. I think some kind of genuine deep transformation in the human condition is in the works. I have no real idea what that will be, but I can smell it in the wind. It's no accident that this historic period is producing people like Mr. Moravec here. Right or wrong, he is a cultural avatar. Maybe we're about to radically change the operating system of the human condition. If so, then this would be a really good time to make backups of our civilization. That's why I want to bring up one last topic today. One last weird, science fictional idea. I call it Deep Archiving. It's possibly the most uncommercial act possible for the cultural institutions we call libraries. I'd like to see stuff archived for the long term. The *very* long term. For the successors of our civilization. Possibly for the successors of the human race.

We're already leaving some impressive gifts for the remote future of this planet. Nuclear wastes, for instance. We're going to be neatly archiving this repulsive trash in concrete blocks and salt mines and fused glass canisters, for tens of thousands of years. Imagine the pleasure of discovering one of these nice radioactive time-bombs six thousand years from now. Imagine the joy of selfless, dedicated archaeologists burrowing into one of these twentieth-century pharaoh's tombs and dropping dead, slowly and painfully. Gosh, thanks ancestors! Thanks, twentieth century! Thanks for thinking of us!

Possibly, it is our moral obligation to explain ourselves to these possible future people that we might possibly offend. Possibly. Shouldn't we give some thought to leaving them a legacy a little less offensive than our giant fossilized landfills and the radioactive fallout layer in the polar snow? If we're going to put the Library of Congress in our hip pocket, I'd like to see us put a Library of Congress beside every canister of nuclear waste. Let's airmail the Library of Congress to the year 20,000 AD.

There's absolutely no benefit for us in this action. There's no money in it. That's why I like the idea. That's why I find it appealing. I think it would be good for the soul of consumer society. It's a moral gesture to demonstrate that our sense of values is not entirely selfish, not entirely narrow, not entirely short-term. I hope you'll think about Deep Archiving. As weird ideas go it's one of the less hazardous and more workable ones. If you remember one idea from my visit here, I hope you'll remember that idea.

David Brin

...prolific science fiction author
Sundiver (1980)
Startide Rising (1983)
The Practice Effect (1984)
The Postman (1985)
The River of Time (1986)
Heart of the Comet (1986, with Gregory Benford)
The Uplift War (1987)
Earth (1990)

...frequently incorporates libraries into his work
(He used the word "library" 57 times in *Startide Rising* and 56 times in
The Uplift War.)

As writers go, I suppose I'm known as a bit of an optimist, so it seems only
natural that this novel projects a future where there's a little more wisdom
than folly ... maybe a bit more hope than despair.

In fact, it's about the most encouraging tomorrow I can imagine right now.

What a sobering thought.
David Brin, *Earth* (New York: Bantam, 1990), preface.

Thinking Robots
an Aware Internet
and
Cyberpunk Librarians

Gaia, Freedom, and Human Nature—Some Ironies on the Way to Creating the Network of the Future

David Brin

It is an honor to be invited to speak before such a distinguished gathering of champions for literacy. I have been asked, before beginning my own remarks, to comment on some of the statements made by my fellow speakers.

First off, I am glad that Bruce Sterling and I agree about Benjamin Franklin, one of my principal heroes. My wife and I named our newborn son after him. Ben Franklin's life story is a lesson in humility for those of us with ambitions to grasp the culture around us. That culture is now much too vast and complicated for one person to encompass, or even adequately sample. Even in Franklin's day, it was already too complex for anyone but a great genius to span. He was the last person, I believe, who read all the great books of his time, had deep conversations with all of the great minds, and dated *all* the interesting women. It's too late now, even for a genius. Our culture is simply too enormous.

Bruce also brought to mind something Garrett Hardin wrote about in his book, *The Tragedy of the Commons*... that there used to be land and other assets which people in communities shared jointly, caring for and utilizing these resources outside of the normal push and shove of a zero-sum, laissez-faire economy. It did not matter that these commons were unprotected, or exempt from the marketplace, back when populations were low and when rigid social sanctions kept people from seeking self-gratification, whatever the cost. But Hardin points out that human nature, plus selfish economic forces, eventually caused people to exploit and then destroy what

35

was shared, so that in time, only that which was protected by being owned, either privately or by governments, had any endurance.

Hardin's point is tragic and poignant. But then, what are we to make of today's Internet? It appears to be the restoration of something very much like the pre-15th century commons!

Who owns the Internet? Who controls it? The answer is... nobody is in charge.

Take those people one occasionally runs across, on the Net, who dislike something they have read, and want it excised. In outrage, they holler— "Why doesn't somebody censor this?"

Who are they talking to? From what hierarchy are they demanding authoritarian redress?

What we see are big institutions, small institutions, and individuals, all paying their connection charges, phone bills or whatever, maintaining the computers and the nodes... and nobody controls the whole. Yet a whole *exists*, a whole which is vastly more competent than the sum of its parts. A lot of companies and educational institutions willingly take a bearable financial loss in order to support this new commons which is expanding inventively everywhere, allowing chat-lines, special interest groups, even anarchists and net-parasites, to join the flow. Why? Because the fruit of this commons—enhanced creativity—is worth whatever it costs.

The glass may be half-empty, given Bruce Sterling's vivid warnings. But is it not half-full, as well? A vibrant underground exists, involving millions of irascibly independent-minded people, and with the complicity of many—though certainly not all—persons at the highest echelons of business, education, and government. The warnings we have just heard are valid, indeed. There *are* dire threats to this commons. But it should be noted *that* the commons exists, a unique and faith-restoring reversal of long-proclaimed historical trends. The commons is not yet dead. We should put high and urgent priority to its nurturance and protection.

My other preliminary comment has to do with Hans Moravec's idea that we—the people in this room, here and now—may actually be simulations. That we might be mental images, as it were, being played out by some far greater mind, or set of minds, in our future.

What an image: We exist, we *are*, because somebody downstream is remembering us.

The idea of being in "reruns"... just like Chevy Chase telling the same jokes about Gerald Ford countless times on late night TV... might be humorous, frightening, or bemusing, depending on your philosophical bent. But what I find exceptional about the notion is—Why us?

Why would great minds of a future time "replay" their Twentieth Century ancestors? Might we be "classics," like the best Marx Brothers movies, or films by Capra, or Sturgess? Perhaps. If we are being remembered right now, perhaps it is because this is/was a crux point in the history of intelligent life on Earth.

The future God-like minds that Hans Moravec spoke of would understand something far better than we do, who are close to the problem. They would understand how difficult it is/was to for a mob of smart animals like ourselves, filled with all sorts of inconvenient, rapacious, insatiable internal drives, to somehow get themselves under control and turn themselves into worthy, grownup custodians of this world. Into beings worthy of descendants who will reach fantastic vistas that we could never imagine.

If we succeed in such an unprecedented endeavor, then we will have been the generation that created a great civilization, filled with possibilities. Why are we being replayed, then? Because quality work is worth replaying!

It may be that meetings such as this one—of librarians in San Francisco, in 1992—are re-run now... I mean in the far future... because those transcendent descendants are riveted by primal, pivotal moments in time.

"How did mere bright animals *do* that?" They wonder, calling up the classic scene once more. "How did they manage to bring about *us?*"

Enough. It was my job, as clean-up hitter, to start with commentary on the other fascinating speakers. Now that is done. On to my prepared remarks.

Life and Information on Earth: Gaia, the Ultimate Computer

Yesterday morning in Southern California, I got up early to prepare for this trip... just in time to experience our biggest earthquake in 50 years. Then I flew to San Francisco! This was smart?

Well, in fact, it showed a remarkable self-confidence in my ability to behave like a god.

To fly through the air, in other words, and land safely. To say "go" to a taxi driver and be transported swiftly to an Elysian tower. To flash a piece of plastic and be given a room, and turn a switch and have light burst forth, and moderately clean water at the touch of a tap.

When I give talks to high school students, I ask them to consider how, in the context of other times, they *are*, in effect, gods. To almost any prior culture, the powers at the command of the average teenager would have been associated with omnipotent beings. The students never think of it that way, because this society has done something unprecedented. It has given god-like power to virtually everybody! It's the most astonishing thing—that we have taken bona fide miracles and made them mundane, even boring.

Yesterday's earthquakes reminded me how frail this situation really is. They reminded me that we live perched on a huge primal, dynamic planet far from equilibrium, relying on its good behavior for our continued existence. If the ocean rose or fell or sloshed, as some people's swimming pools did yesterday, by just two percent, what would happen to us here by the bay? Or if the sun's output climbed by two percent? You all know what it means when your own body's temperature rises or falls by such a tiny fraction.

Each of these are systems which self-regulate far better than our intelligent minds, than our politics, certainly than our economy or the stock market. Self-regulating adaptive systems are all the rage these days. They use feedback loops to maintain a certain amount of stability far from equilibrium—almost a contradiction in terms, until you realize the vast array of systems that do it. Nobel prize-winning physicist Murray Gell-Mann has generalized such self-regulating, adaptive structures to include anything which records and compresses information about itself and its environment, information which can then be used later to perpetuate or reproduce the system.

A prime example would be librarians... at least those of you who have replicated.

Gell-Mann and others demonstrate that most *equilibrium* states are very simple. They have a tendency to be very stable, unlike anything living. (Death is an equilibrium state.) That which is *interesting* has a tendency to exist and behave very far from equilibrium, like a living organism, or the earth's atmosphere, or some of the sophisticated information systems being discussed here today. Such systems tend to be complex, hard to maintain, but also fantastically adaptable.

Many of you have heard of the Gaia hypothesis, which I expand upon shamelessly in my novel, *Earth*. James Lovelock and Lynn Margulis, among others, have promoted the idea that our planet is more than just a complex adaptive system in stable disequilibrium. In effect, it is a living organism, with myriad cells—organs, if you will—made up of its many species and ecosystems. Some have taken the Gaia idea even farther, to the point of stating that humans should be deemed the *brain* of the living planet, because we provide intelligence to that which did not know itself before. (In which case, what brain gives its own body cancer? Or lops off its body's limbs—one way of metaphorically describing the annihilation of our natural environment?)

It is an huge concept, which has caught the imaginations of millions. But then, envisioning grand, unifying wholeness out of disparate parts has always been one of the great egotistical exercises of the western world—at least as important as the much demonized and maligned western tendency toward reductionism. The two trends, synthesis and analysis, have together turned idle daydreaming into the powerful technique: metaphorization.

One of the chief glories and flaws of human nature is our conceited urge to impose simple-minded order on complex systems. Freud did it. Darwin and Marx did it. Each created grand unifying schemes, only one of which survives today as a viable model, because its author willingly subjected his theory of evolution to criticism and experimental verification. The others, thinking themselves saviors of humanity, demanded that their models be taken whole, proving that Freud and Marx were never scientists at all.

It is fun and addictive to construct grand metaphors. Leaders, philosophers, idealists are perpetually building and preaching models of political systems, philosophies, and now the information net of the future. The problem is that we don't like to have these models reproached. We hate criticism. And this leads to a profoundly ironic situation.

Hans Moravec spoke of machines which may someday be able to do thought experiments of a sort, mentally trying out what might happen, before putting actions into effect. Einstein called this process *gedankenexperiment*, and we humans do it all the time. "How will people react if I wear this? How will my boss react if I say that?" High school students do this without ever contemplating how god-like the behavior is to peer, even dimly, into the future. How powerful it would be—if only *everyone else* weren't also doing it, making prediction a delicate, complicated game of outguessing one another.

People often speak of the wisdom of error, the willingness to take chances and make mistakes. But it has a second side. Mistakes can also be deadly, especially for societies. Any system for handling information and reaching decisions must certainly take chances, but it must also have good techniques for minimizing the rate of error, when it finally acts.

To illustrate the implications, let me relate to you something that I call the Parable of the Peacock.

What is good for the male peacock? What benefits his overall success in life?

A huge flashy tail.

Is this garish appendage good for the *race* of peacocks? No. It makes them slow, cumbersome, easy to catch. Yet the tails have burgeoned with each bird generation.

Clearly, in this case what dominates is what benefits the individual. The process of sexual selection assures this.

Now, what is good for a *leader*, in a nation, business or group? What have most leaders throughout history spent much of their time and energy doing? Suppressing criticism. Criticism, by its very nature, makes things tough for leaders.

Oh, the number of times George Washington was tempted to crack down, like all of his predecessors. However, unlike those others, Washington had reached an astounding insight. He knew that *criticism is the only known antidote to error*. It is the only reliable way by which mistakes are avoided, by philosophers, by states, by individuals. This conflict of interest, between what serves society and what serves individual leaders, is one of the greatest quandaries facing humanity in its efforts to create systems which might be self-sustaining and sane. Like the tragedy of the commons, it is a problem worthy of deep, mature reflection.

(Noisy, irritating criticism was what made the difference between a one billion dollar fiasco in western Pennsylvania, called Three Mile Island, and a titanic catastrophe in the Ukraine, called Chernobyl. "Oh, we'll add those three extra pumps," the power utility said, before the accident. "But just to make you idiot environmentalists happy. Of course we'll never actually need them.")

This dichotomy between the needs of leaders and the good of the commonwealth puts in new perspective what Washington, and Franklin, and Jefferson were after by setting down deep principles of freedom of speech.

Freedom of speech is not a gift from on high. It was not declared by God. It is not holy, or even natural. No other human society ever practiced it. Even we, who are loony enough to consider it sacred, don't practice it very well. Yet, although it runs against every tyrannical impulse of human nature... impulses to suppress whatever that loudmouth fool over there is saying... the fact is that we *try* to live by it. Not because free speech is holy, or natural, but because it works. Because it is pragmatic. Because it allows the rapid generation of a multitude of ideas, most of which are chaff, and then allows those notions to be criticized by *other* egotistical people, so that a fair percentage of the best ideas rise, and most garbage eventually sinks.

In other words, free speech encourages criticism, like a human body's immune system, to seek out and attack possibly cancerous or fatal ideas. Those which survive open debate are (at least in theory) those which deserve to thrive.

Naturally, any attempt by leaders or public institutions to pre-judge or pre-approve concepts will be self-defeating. Decrees by aristocrats or intellectuals or demagogues will always be less efficient than the free interplay of ideas. If you doubt this, try picking and choosing which antibodies your immune system would produce!

Now, all of this obviously applies to the future of the information network evolving at conferences such as this one. Like the sun, the earth, and the human body, in the long run, stability is achieved not by laws or rules, but through self-regulating, adaptive systems that allow large forces to balance each other out. In this case, in the World Information Net, this balance will be driven by the power of ten billion voices, ten trillion ideas.

Such a system *cannot* be designed in detail, but the right mix of basic elements can be planned in advance, to keep it healthy so that this maelstrom of ideas and myths will be *fecund* in its creation of vast quantities of metaphors, but also *sane* enough to ultimately reject bad notions in a fair market, clearing the way for new ones to take their place.

One principal element must be openness. In the human body, nutrients must flow, and white blood cells have to reach their targets. In the Net of tomorrow, the light of criticism must shine everywhere, or secrets which lay hidden will fester into new crises, new weapons, new errors.

In an information society, secrecy is the equivalent of cancer.

The Privacy Scam... and Other Quandaries

With the ultimate goal of a sane, healthy Net in mind, I would like to address several issues which I see looming in the years ahead. Issues I foresee as critical to the future of the information society.

If secrecy is the greatest threat to an open, error-detecting, egalitarian World Net, then the one of the most ignoble scams being foisted upon the American people right now is that of *data privacy*. It is, arguably, the latest attempt by aristocratism to stage a quiet coup and to take over tomorrow's leading source of wealth and power—information.

Let me explain. Throughout human history, almost every civilization has been pyramidal in its social structure. It appears to be basic to human nature—at least until we someday become fully mature—for those who have achieved success to seek positions at the pinnacle of society, and then connive to impede others from reaching those same heights. Even if we are proud of having become rich in an egalitarian context, by providing quality goods and services in a fair market, we nevertheless are tempted to use our wealth and leverage to manipulate the system, so that our children will exert unearned power over other people's children.

Mind you, I have every intention of striving to achieve wealth, myself. When it is open and fair, the incentive-based free market achieves miracles of innovation and productivity unparalleled by any other. My point here is to demonstrate yet another quandary of human nature, like *The Tragedy of the Commons* and the antagonism of leaders toward criticism, which society must overcome if we are to survive and thrive. It is very difficult for a rich man to do like Andrew Carnegie, and create monuments instead of dynasties. Monuments open and beneficial to all, such as Carnegie's famed libraries. Until all who achieve such heights think that way, so long as insatiability and aristocratism are temptations to an insecure but powerful class, the market will always contain a potentially deadly flaw.

The latest attempt by an aristocratic order to stage a coup consists, in large part, of *privacy laws*. And it is working. It makes wonderfully effective propaganda to tell people—"You don't want snoops looking through your private records, do you? So let's have legislation to protect them!" This position is rapidly becoming as unassailable as apple pie... and certainly much safer than motherhood.

But let me ask a simple question—Do you honestly think that any privacy law is going to keep high officials, like George Bush, or billionaires, like H. Ross Perot, from finding out anything and everything they want to know about you? No privacy act will ever prevent the rich and powerful from snooping about you. All such laws accomplish is to prevent *you* from finding out about *them*.

What is the solution? We don't want our current bank records on public display, and legitimate businesses certainly do need to safeguard their valuable trade practices. I don't know the answer to this quandary, but some options have been proposed. One possibility is to allow anyone to keep secrets for up to ten years. That's plenty of time for most business cycles and private needs.

The effects might go far beyond simply opening the system to freer flow of information and avoidance of error. It may also positively affect public and private ethics. Can you think of anything from ten years ago you'd be ashamed to have revealed?

Well, all right, let's rephrase that! Let's say you had *warning*... if you knew that, ten years from now, anything you did today might become public knowledge, wouldn't you strive to behave just a little better? It sounds chilling, at first. But in fact, this would only replicate the way things were in old tribes, or in small towns, where secrets lasted only a little while, and everyone knew all about everyone else. Don't we tend to look back nostalgically on the honesty and courtesy of such times? Might true openness, tearing down the castle walls of isolation, help restore the village for a world of rootless citizens of megalopolis?

Now I can see some of you, who were looking stunned just a moment ago, are starting to smile. Yes, you're right. I am being provocative on purpose. It's my job, after all, to stir around in the pot of ideas, looking for amazing things.

No, I'm not saying that all computer passwords should be abandoned tomorrow, followed by locks on all doors and then the clothes on our backs! But I do think somebody needs at last to speak to the other side of this issue, so that we don't simply march en masse into the future to the tune of some aristocratic drum.

So much for issue number one—the scam illusion of privacy. Just watch out for it. Think about it for yourselves.

Issue number two is the problem of *access*.

My wife and I have just returned from a year and a half living in France. It was a fascinating experience, learning about another culture, another history, another set of assumptions about the world. Most fascinating for a person like me was to be forced to speak awkwardly in a language that made me seem as articulate as a four-year old. It was a useful exercise in humility.

But I want to address something about the French national character. While as individuals they are fanatically individualistic, en masse they have always been elitists. The chief effect of their revolution was to switch from an inherited aristocracy to a meritocratic one in which examinations and the Grandes Écoles (universities) determine who gets to be God. For example the French accept the idea of a government committee declaring by fiat what their information network shall be like.

The interesting result is that a *third* to *half* of all the homes in France now have Minitel—the French equivalent of Compuserve—and they use it. (The first ones were given out free, and you need no modem or expertise to use one.) Most people no longer use paper phone directories. Everything from rail tickets to opera schedules, to chat-lines and weather is available. We used Minitel all the time in Paris, far more than I access the Net today, back in America.

The irony is that, because of an elitist, doctrinaire decision, the spread of this technology has been far more pervasive throughout France, and far more democratic. Here in this country, just a few percent use the Net in its varied corporate and academic incarnations. The North American system is vastly more complex, more capable, more disorganized and frenzied, and more free. But it is also effectively far *less* egalitarian.

This strange result parallels the crisis in American education, in which the great benefits of chaotic, extravagant freedom accrue to the very top students, those capable of taking advantage of the smorgasbord of opportunities around them, while the rest of their peers learn much less than French students, who study by rote and memorization. It is a classic quandary between two ways of looking at the world, at information, and at the question of "access." I do not believe that it *should* be a situation pitting excellence against equality, freedom against justice, but so far that is just one more of the many paradoxes before us, which we must solve if we are to achieve our goals.

Courtesy. Many of you have seen this phenomenon on nearly every info-network—people "flaming on," spewing diatribes, in effect screaming ASCII invective at anyone who disagrees with their point of view. It is not a new phenomenon, but one we encounter whenever a new medium of communication appears. Radio dramatically amplified the perceived power and charisma of such early, hypnotic users as Huey Long and Adolf Hitler, and it conveyed a myriad of unchallenged lies. Until a populace learns sophistication—and develops calluses—any new field of discourse can be rife with dangers. Or at minimum plagued with discourtesy.

What happens in our new medium is that the screen in front of the user provides few, if any, of the social interaction cues that we learned as children, and that evolved over thousands of years. These consist of body language, facial expressions, and continuing feedback from others. These cues enabled our ancestors to gauge how to say things in tribal council in ways that generally did not cause the guy two rocks over to pick up a spear and drive it through your belly. None of this is taking place on today's home computer screen.

Instead, what you see is people behaving like they have Tourette's Syndrome, the mental ailment which causes its hapless victims to suddenly, uncontrollably, burst into fits of extravagant cursing. These "Net-Tourettes" —or flamers—are a bane to the new commons. They are a threat to our ability to create a citizenship, a sense of *polis*, out of the burgeoning information community. Something must be done about it.

Yet, of course, the solution absolutely cannot come from on high! It cannot come as censorship in any form, or the free market of ideas we spoke of earlier will be impaired, perhaps ruined. Rather, what we need is new interfaces that are much better at giving the sorts of feedback (e.g., facial expressions) that people are already tuned to heed. This trend toward humanizing the medium began with the Macintosh and will grow more natural with each generation of equipment and software. It cannot help doing so, for customers will demand it.

But the ultimate solution will not arise out of simply improved interfaces. In the free exchange of a true network, there will inevitably develop certain types of feedback that cause cyber-sociopaths to *fear* behaving too obnoxiously toward their neighbors. As in real life, where repeated odious public behavior can lead to a punch in the nose, this feedback is going to manifest itself in pain. No law or supervising agency will enforce this more powerfully than peer pressure, applied in imaginative ways.

In my novel, *Earth*, I describe something called a "courtesy worm." It is a guerilla program, an illegal virus, that goes around targeting people who are too angry and vituperative on the Net. Attracted by unsavory, scatological, and ad hominem phrasings, the worm gets into the flamer's system and announces, "Hello. You have been infected by the program, *Emilypost*, because your presence on the Net is impinging on the rights and enjoyment of others. If you'll check your credibility ratings, sir, you would soon realize nobody is listening to you, anyway. We suggest you try behaving in a more grown up manner. If you don't, you will soon discover certain features of *Emilypost* which..."

I am not advocating this "solution." It is, simply, inevitable.

The concept of "credibility ratings" is another one deserving discussion. What if politicians and announcers on television, had the equivalent of *Consumer Reports* believability ratings displayed underneath their images, whenever they took to the screen? What if the Net, in its feedback loops, provided such a statistical tag next to the icon of each member-citizen who chimed up with an idea? Would that improve the efficiency of the metaphor-generating-culling system? Or would it turn into tyranny by the masses... a homogenizing oppression by the majority? I don't know. But it might be an idea worth further exploration.

Hans Moravec raised another interesting issue. What to do when computers get smart... even much smarter than us? This is a concept that's been debated in science fiction for a long time. Unless you believe physicist Roger Penrose (author of *The Emperor's New Mind*), machines are destined to get very, very powerful. What shall we do when our creations far surpass us?

Well, Isaac Asimov, bless his memory, came up with his famous three laws of robotics—and I'm sure many of you are familiar with them—which would supposedly be deeply ingrained to control robotic behavior at the most fundamental level, excluding forever any behaviors which might be contrary to the good of human beings. With all due respect to the good doctor, I have to say that is a no-go solution. Once they get smart, some computers will *become lawyers*, and we all know that lawyers find ways of interpreting things their own way, no matter what. This was pointed out beautifully by one of the greatest science fiction authors of all time, Jack Williamson, who showed that robots programmed to "serve" us might (1) decide to "serve" us for dinner, or (2) decide that service means protection, and protection means preventing us from taking any risks at all.

("No, no, don't use that knife, you might hurt yourself." Then, a generation later, "No, no, don't use that fork." Then, "Don't use that spoon. Just sit on this pillow and we'll do everything for you.")

There *is* a way of handling your creations so that they are likely to be loyal to you, even if they're much more intelligent. It's a tried and true method that has worked for quite a few million people who created entities smarter than themselves in times past. The technique is to raise them as members of our civilization. *Raise them as our children.*

There is every reason to believe that such brilliant entities will *have* to be raised that way, because of something we discussed much earlier—the wisdom of error. In other words, they will not be prim and perfect, like movie robots, because perfection is death. Death to flexibility and death to ideas. Instead, truly intelligent machines will have to, as children do, stumble before walking. They will, perforce, try out countless stupid things, even after they learn to use realistic thought experiments to avoid the worst errors.

So I have faith that, even when our computers become smarter than us, the best of them will still come home, take us out fishing, and excitedly try to explain to us what they're doing for a living. And, like countless other generations of good parents dazzled by their brilliant offspring, we'll say, "That's all right, son. I don't understand, but I'm sure you're going to make us proud. Now say, did you hear the latest lawyer joke?"

Will events outrace our wisdom? That is always a central—perhaps the crucial—question, especially when discussing a new technology.

Ever since the discovery of gunpowder, and even before that, the power for individuals to destroy, to do harm, has spread and democratized and reached more hands than literacy and self-restraint. Today we are distributing knowledge and power so widely, to millions of people, that the amazing thing isn't how many die of violence, but that cavemen with automatic weapons slaughter each other on the streets so seldom!

Will we continue to be so lucky when the secrets of Los Alamos and Atomagorsk are declassified and released onto the Net? (This isn't far fetched. Most of the relevant information is already loose, and who will be the one to say we should gather it up, to sweep back in the bottle?) The Net had *better* be healthy, critical, open, since it will carry vast amounts of dangerous stuff.

I have confidence that an open commons, a true commonwealth of ideas, will be able to handle any crisis, as I tried to depict in *Earth*. But, then, I'm also known as the "optimist of science fiction." It's a good thing to have Bruce Sterling on the same platform, with his trumpeting alarum of danger, lest my pollyanna visions of glasses half-full lullaby you to complacency. Half-empty, after all, is too empty by far.

If I sound like an optimist, it's because I see optimism as an ecological niche that I get to fill, almost alone, in a world full of pessimists. But catch me in my darker moments, and you may hear another tune.

I have been to Easter Island, and left there a changed man. No place on earth offers a better parallel, a better *parable* for the choices we face in the decades ahead. Despite all the romantic, multiculturalist propaganda you hear today, most past civilizations did not admire or work well with the environment. In a recent book, *A Forest Journey*, the author, John Perlin, describes how virtually every human civilization despoiled its environment. It is part of human nature, part of *animal* nature, to seek individual, short term advantage at the cost of the commons. The forces of evolution seem arrayed against a happy ending for civilization or the planet.

On Easter Island, the original Polynesian inhabitants arrived at paradise, a beautiful forested land where birds didn't even run away when humans walked up with clubs. Within a few generations, every tree had been felled. All the native birds were extinct. The people kept chickens, and had taro root... and they ate each other. Is it any wonder?

Visitors to Easter Island say—"Ooh, how did they chip those great stone statues? How did they move them? Was it UFOs? ESP?"

I think those are terribly demeaning and patronizing questions. Ingenious humans can do just about anything they set their minds to. If you were a descendant of the folk who ignorantly, negligently despoiled the island, and if you got it into your head that chipping those forlorn, despairing images might somehow get you *off* of this godawful place that your parents left you, I'm sure you'd find ways of chipping and moving stone!

So might our own descendants, if we leave them a desolation.

Easter Island is a parable to us because what the native Polynesians accomplished with stone tools, over many generations, with a few people, to a fragile ecosystem, we are now doing with five billion people and chain saws and great ingenuity to the most resilient, self-organizing, self-regulating ecosystem of all ... the entire planet. Taking it swiftly toward a state of equilibrium. And equilibrium is death.

But then, optimism creeps out of my heart, my soul. No other culture before ours has had the habit, learned the hard way over centuries, of teaching its children to criticize, to seek out what is wrong and declaim it. What other society would have noticed or cared about something as obscure and abstract as a hole in the ozone layer, above the far-off Antarctic, except a culture wise enough to train some of its offspring to be bright, eager, well-funded gadflies? What other civilization ever worried so, day in day out, in unending efforts to find errors?

In other words, just when it may be too late, we have started poking sticks in this ground before us to find out where the quicksand is. A fine example is found in meetings such as this one, in which librarians, heroes in the preservation and democratic conveyance of knowledge, gather to worry about how to implement a sane Net. The result of this and a myriad gatherings like it may be solutions to the quandaries I posed this afternoon... and all the others standing between us and a living, thriving, self-aware planet.

This is why there is hope. We are thinking. We are doing thought experiments about the future. We're trying to figure it out.

In the end, the Sane Network is not going to emerge from some committee, but from all of us, by tossing up idea after idea and recognizing that ninety-nine percent of them will be garbage, like so many you've heard this afternoon. But in the end, out of the dross, there will shine gold.

Thinking Robots...

The Three Laws of Robotics

First Law: A robot may not injure a human being, or, through inaction, allow a human being to come to harm.

Second Law: A robot must obey the orders given it by human beings except where such orders would conflict with the First Law.

Third Law: A robot must protect its own existence as long as such protection does not conflict with the First and Second Law.
  Isaac Asimov, *Robot Visions* (New York: Penguin Books, 1990), 407.

Who's gonna make us follow these rules?

Thinking Robots
An Aware Internet
and
Cyberpunk Librarians

Letter from Moravec to Penrose

Hans Moravec

Carnegie Mellon University

Date: 9 Feb 90 02::02:22 GMT
From: Hans.Moravec@rover.ri.cmu.edu
Subject: Dear Roger,
Newsgroups: sci.nanotech

This is an open letter, distribute at will.
Comments are solicited. Thanks.—Hans Moravec

To: Professor Roger Penrose, Department of Mathematics, Oxford, England

Dear Professor Penrose,

Thank you for sharing your thoughts on thinking machinery in your new book *The Emperor's New Mind*, and in the February 1 *New York Review of Books* essay on my book *Mind Children*. I've been a fan of your mathematical inventions since my high school days in the 1960s, and was intrigued to hear that you had written an aggressively titled book about my favorite subject. I enjoyed every part of that book—the computability chapters were an excellent review, the phase space view of entropy was enlightening, the Hilbert space discussion spurred me on to another increment in my incredibly protracted amateur working through of Dirac, and I'm sure we both learned form the chapter on brain anatomy. You won't be surprised to learn, however, that I found your overall argument wildly wrong headed!

If your book was written to counter a browbeating you felt from proponents of hard AI, mine was inspired by the browbeaten timidity I found in the majority of my colleagues in that community. As the words "frightening" and "nightmare" in your review suggest, intelligent machines are an emotion-stirring prospect, and it is hard to remain unbrowbeaten in the face

51

of frequent hostility. But why hostility? Our emotions were forged over eons of evolution, and are triggered by situations, like threats to life or territory, that resemble those that influenced our ancestors' reproductive success. Since there were no intelligent machines in our past, they must resemble something else to incite such a panic—perhaps another tribe down the stream poaching in our territory, or a stronger, smarter rival for our social position, or a predator that will carry away our offspring in the night. But is it reasonable to allow our actions and opportunities to be limited by spurious resemblances and unexamined fears? Here's how I look at the question. We are in the process of creating a new kind of life. Though utterly novel, this new life form resembles us more than it resembles anything else in the world. To earn their keep in society, robots are being taught our skills. In the future, as they work among us on an increasingly equal footing, they will acquire our values and goals as well—robot software that causes antisocial behavior, for instance, would soon cease being manufactured. How should we feel about beings that we bring into the world, that are similar to ourselves, that we teach our way of life, that will probably inherit the world when we are gone? I consider them our children. As such they are not fundamentally threatening, though they will require careful upbringing to instill in them a good character. Of course, in time, they will outgrow us, create their own goals, make their own mistakes, and go their own way, with us perhaps a fond memory. But that is the way of children. In America, at least, we consider it desirable for offspring to live up to their maximum potential and to exceed their parents.

You fault my book for failing to present alternatives to the "hard AI" position. It is my honest opinion that there are no convincing scientific alternatives. There are religious alternatives, based on subjective premises about a special relation of man to the universe, and there are flawed secular rationalizations of anthropocentrism. The two alternatives you offer, namely John Searle's philosophical argument and your own physical speculation, are of the latter kind. Searle's position is that a system that, however accurately, simulates the processes in a human brain, whether with marks on paper of signals in a computer, is a "mere imitation" of thought, not thought itself. Pejorative labels may be an important tool for philosophy professors, but they don't create reality. I imagine a future debate in which Professor Searle, staunch to the end, succumbs to the "mere imitation" of thought and emotion. Your own position is that some physical principle in human brains produces "non-computable" results, and that somehow this leads to consciousness. Well, I agree, but the same principle works equally well for robots, and it's not nearly as mysterious as you suggest.

Alan Turing's computability arguments, now more than fifty years old, were a perfect fit to David Hilbert's criteria for the mechanization of deductive mathematics, but they don't define the capabilities of a robot or a human. They assume a closed process working from a fixed, finite, amount of initial information. Each step of a Turing machine computation can at best preserve this information, and may destroy a bit of it, allowing the computation to eventually "run down," like a closed physical system whose entropy increases. The simple expedient of opening the computation to external information voids this suffocating premise, and with it the uncomputability theorems. For instance, Turing, proved the uncomputability of most numbers, since there are only countably many machine programs, and uncountably many real numbers for them to generate. But it is trivial to produce "uncomputable" numbers with a Turing machine, if the machine is augmented with a true randomizing device. Whenever another digit of the number is needed, the randomizer is consulted, and the result written on the appropriate square of the tape. The emerging number is drawn uniformly from a real interval, and thus (with probability 1) is an "uncomputable" number. The randomizing device allows the machine to make an unlimited number of unpredetermined choices, and is an unbounded information source. In a Newtonian universe, where every particle has an infinitely precise position and momentum, fresh digits could be extracted from finer and finer discriminations of the initial conditions by the amplifying effects of chaos, as in a ping pong ball lottery machine. A quantum mechanical randomizer might operate by repeatedly confining a particle to a tiny space, so fixing its position and undefining its momentum, then releasing it and registering whether it travels left or right. Just where the information flows from in this case is one of the mysteries of quantum mechanics.

The above constitutes a basic existence proof for "uncomputable" results in real machines. A more interesting example is the augmentation of a "Hilbert" machine that systematically generates inferences from an initial set of axioms. As your book recounts, a deterministic device of this kind will never arrive at some true consequences of the axioms. But suppose the machine, using a randomizer, from time to time concocts an entirely new statement, and adds it to the list of inferences. If the new "axiom" (or hypothesis) is inconsistent with the original set, then sooner or later the machine will generate an inference of "FALSE" from it. If that happens the machine backtracks and deletes the inconsistent hypothesis and all of its inferences, then invents a new hypothesis in its place. Eventually some of the surviving hypotheses will be unprovable theorems of the original axiom system, and the overall system will be an idiosyncratic, "creative" extension of the original one. Consistency is never assured, since a contradiction could turn up at any time, but the older hypotheses are less and less likely to be rescinded. Mathematics made of humans has the same property. Even when an axiomatic system is proved consistent, the augmented system in which the proof takes place could itself be inconsistent, invalidating the proof!

When humans (and future robots) do mathematics they are less likely to draw inspiration from rolls of dice than by observing the world around them. The real world too is a source of fresh information, but pre-filtered by physics and evolution, saving us some work. When our senses detect a regularity (let's say, spherical soap bubbles) we can form a hypothesis (e.g., that spheres enclose volume with the least area) likely to be consistent with hypotheses we already hold, since they too were abstracted from the real world, and the real world is probably consistent. This brings me to your belief in a Platonic mathematical reality, which I also think you make unnecessarily mysterious. The study of formal systems shows there is nothing fundamentally unique about the particular axioms and rules of inference we use in our thinking. Other systems of strings and rewriting rules look just as interesting on paper. They may not correspond to any familiar kind of language or thought, but it is easy to construct machines (and presumably animals) to act on their strange dictates. In the course of evolution (which, significantly, is driven by random mutations) minds with unusual axioms or inference structures must have arisen from time to time. But they did poorly in the contest for survival and left no descendants. In this way we were shaped by an evolutionary game of twenty questions—the intuitions we harbor are those that work in this place. The Platonic reality you sense is the groundrules of the physical universe in which you evolved—not just its physics and geometry but its logic. If there are other universes with different rules, other Roger Penroses may be sensing quite different Platonic realities.

And now to that other piece of mysticism, human consciousness. Three centuries ago Rene Descartes was a radical. Having observed the likes of clockwork ducks and the imaging properties of bovine eyes, he rejected the vitalism of his day and suggested that the body was just a complex machine. But lacking a mechanical model for thought, he exorcised the spirit of life only as far as a Platonic realm of mind somewhere beyond the pineal gland—a half-measure that gave us centuries of fruitless haggling on the "mind-body" problem. Today we do have mechanical models for thought, but the Cartesian tradition still lends respectability to a fantastic alternative that comforts anthropocentrists, but explains nothing. Your own proposal merely substitutes "mysterious unexplained physics" for spirit. The center of Descartes' ethereal domain was consciousness, the awareness of thought —"I think therefore I am."

 You say you have no definition for consciousness, but think you know it when you see it, and you think you see it in your housepets. So, a dog looks into your eyes with its big brown ones, tilts its head, lifts an ear and whines softly, and you feel that there is someone there. I suppose, from your published views, that those same actions from a future robot would meet with a less charitable interpretation. But suppose the robot also addressed you in a pained voice, saying "Please, Roger, it bothers me that you don't think of me as a real person. What can I do to convince you? I am aware of you, and I am aware of myself. And I tell you, your rejection is almost unbearable." This performance is not a recording, nor is it due to mysterious physics. It is a consequence of a particular organization of the robot's controlling computers and software. The great bulk of the robot's mentality is straightforward and "unconscious." There are processes that reduce sensor data to abstract descriptions for problem solving modules, and other processes that translate the recommendations of the problem solvers into robot actions. But sitting on top of, and sometimes interfering with, all this activity is a relatively small reflective process that receives a digest of sensor data organized as a continuously updated map, or cartoon-like image, of the robot's surroundings. The map includes a representation of the robot itself, with a summary of the robot's internal state, including reports of activity and success or trouble, and even a simplified representation of the reflective process. The process maintains a recent history of this map, like frames of a movie film, and a problem solver programmed to monitor activity in it. One of the reflective process' most important functions is to protect against endless repetitions. The unconscious process for unscrewing a jar lid, for instance, will rotate a lid until it comes free. But if the screw thread is damaged, the attempt could go on indefinitely. The reflective process monitors recent activity for such dangerous deadlocks and interrupts them. As a special case of this, it detects protracted inaction. After a period of quiescence the process begins to examine its map and internal state, particularly the trouble reports, and invokes problem solvers to suggest actions that might improve the situation.

 The Penrose house robot has a module that observes and reasons about the mental state of its master (advertising slogan: "Our Robots Care!"). For reasons best known to its manufacturer, this particular model registers trouble whenever the psychology module infers that the master does not believe the robot is conscious. One slow day the reflective process stirs, and notes a major trouble report of this kind. It runs the human interaction problem solver to find an ameliorating strategy. This produces a plan to initiate a pleading conversation with Roger, with nonverbal cues. So the robot trundles up, stares with its big brown eyes, cocks its head, and begins to speak. To protect its reputation, the manufacturer has arranged it so the robot cannot knowingly tell a lie. Every statement destined for the speech generator is first interpreted and tested by the reflective module. If the robot wishes to say "The window is open," the reflective process checks its map to see if the window is indeed labeled "open." If the information is missing, the process invokes a problem solver, which may produce a sensor strategy that will appropriately update the map. Only if the statement is so verified does the reflective process allow it to be spoken. Otherwise the generating module is itself flagged as troublesome, in a complication that doesn't concern this argument. The solver has generated "Please, Roger, it bothers me that you don't think of me as a real person." The reflective process parses this, and notes, in the map's schematic model of the robot's internals, that the trouble report from the psychology module was generated because of the master's (inferred) disbelief. So the statement is true, and thus spoken. "What can I do to convince you?"-like invoking problem solvers, asking questions sometimes produces solutions, so no lie here. "I am aware of you, and I am aware of myself"—the reflective process refers to its map, and indeed finds a representation of Roger there, and of the robot itself, derived from sensor data, so this statement is true. "And I tell you, your rejection is almost unbearable"—trouble reports carry intensity numbers, and because of the manufacturer's peculiar priorities, the "unconscious robot" condition generates ever bigger intensities. Trouble of too high an intensity triggers a safety circuit that shuts down the robot. The reflective process tests the trouble against the safety limit, and indeed finds that it is close, so this statement also is true. [In case you feel this scenario is far fetched, I am enclosing a recent paper by Steven Vere and Timothy Bickmore of the Lockheed AI center in Palo Alto that describes a working program with its basic elements. They avoid the difficult parts of the robot by working in a simulated world, but their program has a reflective module, and acts and speaks with consciousness of its actions.]

Human (and even canine) consciousness undeniably has subtleties not found in the above story. So will future robots. But some animals (including most of our ancestors) get by with less. A famous example is the Sphex wasp, which paralyzes caterpillars and deposits them in an underground hatching burrow. Normally she digs a burrow, seals the entrance, and leaves to find a caterpillar. Returning, she drops the victim, reopens the entrance, then turns to drag in the prey. But if an experimenter interrupts by moving the caterpillar a short distance away while the wasp is busy at the opening, she repeats the motions of opening the (already open) burrow, after shifting the prey back. If the experimenter again intervenes, she repeats again, and again and again, until either the wasp or the experimenter drops from exhaustion.

Apparently Sphex has no reflective module to detect the cycle. It's not a problem in her simple, stereotyped life, malicious experimenters being rare. But in more complex niches, opportunities for potentially fatal loops must be more frequent and unpredictable. The evolution of consciousness may have started with a "watchdog" circuit guarding against this hazard.

I like thinking about the universe's exotic possibilities, for instance about computers that use quantum superposition to do parallel computations. But even with the additional element of time travel (!), I've never encountered a scheme that gives more than an exponential speedup, which would have tremendous practical consequences, but little effect on computability theorems. Or perhaps the universe is like the random axiomatic system extender described above. When a measurement is made and a wave function collapses, an alternative has been chosen. Perhaps this constitutes an axiomatic extension of the universe—today's rules were made by past measurements, while today's measurements, consistent with the old rules, add to them, producing a richer set for the future.

But robot construction does not demand deep thought about such interesting questions, because the requisite answers already exist in us. Rather than being something entirely new, intelligent robots will be ourselves in new clothing. It took a billion years to invent the concept of a body, of seeing, moving and thinking. Perhaps fundamentals like space and time took even longer to form. But while it may be hard to construct the arrow of perceived time from first principles, it is easy to build a thermostat that responds to past temperatures, and affects those of the future. Somehow, without great thought on our part, the secret of time is passed on to the device. Robots began to see, move and think almost from the moment of their creation. They inherited that from us.

In the nineteenth century the most powerful arithmetic engines were in the brains of human calculating prodigies, typically able to multiply two 10 digit numbers in under a minute. Calculating machinery surpassed them by 1930. Chess is a richer arena, involving patterns and strategy more in tune with our animal skills. In 1970 the best chess computer played at an amateur level, corresponding to a US chess federation rating of about 1500. By 1980 there was a machine playing at a 1900 rating, Expert level. In 1985, a machine (HiTech) at my own university had achieved a Master level of 2300. Last year a different machine from here (Deep Thought) achieved Grandmaster status with a rating of 2500. In past each doubling of chess computer speed raised the quality of its play by about 100 rating points. The Deep Thought team has been adopted by IBM and is constructing a machine on the same principles, but 1000 times as fast. Though Kasparov doubted it on the occasion of defeating Deep Thought in two games last year, his days of absolute superiority are numbered. I estimated in my book that the most developed parts of human mentality—perception, motor control and the common sense reasoning processes—will be matched by machines in no less than 40 years. But many of the skills employed by mathematics professors are more like chess than like common sense. Already I find half of my mathematics not in my head but in the steadily improving Macsyma and Mathematica symbolic mathematics programs that I've used almost daily for 15 years. Sophomoric arguments about the indefinite superiority of man over machine are unlikely to change this trend.

Well, thank you for a stimulating book. As I said in the introduction, I enjoyed every part of it, and its totality compelled me to put into these words ideas that might otherwise have been lost.

Very Best Wishes,
Hans Moravec
Robotics Institute,
Carnegie Mellon University,
Pittsburgh, PA 15213 USA
Arpanet: hpm@rover.ri.cmu.edu
Fax: (412) 682-1793
Telephone: (412) 268-3829

Hans Moravec is a renowned thinker and researcher in the fields of artificial intelligence and robotics. His work is cited frequently throughout this publication. He is one of the speakers at the 1992 LITA President's Program. This letter was widely distributed over the Internet. Internet: Hans. Moravec@rover.ri.cmu.edu

Exotechnology:
Human Efforts To Evolve Beyond *Human Being*

Mel Seesholtz

The Pennsylvania State University

Philosopher of science Thomas Kuhn called it a *paradigm*. Cultural historian Thomas Berry called it a *Story*. Bionomicist Michael Rothschild called it *a mental model of how the world works*. Whatever you call it, in the 20th century, scientific discoveries and technological advances have been so profound, so numerous and have evolved so rapidly that we have not had enough time to create one consistent with what we know, scientifically, and can do, technologically.

Yet in all its versions, there is a consistent theme: *human* efforts to evolve out of, beyond human *being* and the limitations of flesh-and-blood mortal existence. Virtually all religions—Story tellers par excellence—include this self-guided evolution in their mythology and metaphors. In the three Western monotheistic religions, humans evolve post-biologically, post-mortem. Heaven. Medical science attempts to postpone *that* evolution as long as possible. Some of today's **exotechnologies** seek to replace *post-mortem* with *post-biological*.

Virtual Reality

We have all been creating and participating in electronic Virtual Realities virtually all our lives. When you telephone someone, your voice enters cyberspace (the electronic information matrix) and creates **VRs**: **V**oice **R**ealities. Television offers **V**isual **R**ealities. Everyday life is a matrix of **V**isceral **R**ealities. The technology known as *Virtual Reality* attempts to combine **V**oice **R**eality with **V**isual **R**ealities in computer generated interactive simulations of **V**isceral **R**ealities.

Virtual Reality refers to an interface technology. Originally, it was the name Jaron Lanier gave to his company's "artificial reality" technology. It has since become the generic label for 3-D realtime immersion simulation technologies. These metaforms have their mechanical roots in Mort Helig's Sensurama and their electronic roots in military flight simulators. But it was William Gibson's 1984 novel *Neuromancer* which gave *cyberspace* its name and identified its *cyberpunk* ecology.

As a label, "Cyberpunk" is perfection. It suggests the apotheosis of postmodernism. On the one hand, pure negation: of manners, history, philosophy, politics, body, will, affect, anything mediated by cultural memory; on the other, pure attitude: all is power, and "subculture," and the grace of Hip negotiating the splatter of consciousness as it slams against the hard-tech future, the techno-future of artificial immanence, where all that was once nature is simulated and elaborated by technical means, a future world-construct that is as remote from the "lessons of history" as the present mix-up is from the pitiful science fiction fantasies of the past that tried to imagine us.—Istvan Csicsery-Ronay

The significance of the "Cyberpunk Controversy" ... [is] really of two natures: first, the relatively narrow significance of the role cyberpunk has played (and continues to play) in the recent evolution of science fiction into a literary genre of considerable formal ingenuity and thematic significance; secondly, broader significance of c-p's relationship to the complex set of radical ruptures—both within a dominant culture and aesthetic and also within the new social and economic media system (or "postindustrial society") in which we live—that are associated with post-modernism, as that term is being used by critics such as Jean-Francois Lyotard, Ihab Hassan, Jean Baudrilliard.—Larry McCaffrey

Although VR is still in its infancy, potentially the technology represents a new medium for human communication, education and entertainment. VR arcades are already a reality: playtime costs $1.00 per minute. Virtual cadavers help future doctors explore the human body. And cyberpunks are busy exploring the technology's and the metaphor's communicative, mindexpanding possibilities. Their individual and collective efforts fill the electronic screens of the WELL (Whole Earth Lectronic Link) and the glossy pages of *Mondo 2000*, a cybernetic-psychedelic quarterly (Editor-in-Chief, R.U. Sirius; Domineditrix, Queen Mu) published by Fun City Media, Berkeley, California.

Although they have improved dramatically in the last few years, VR simulations are not yet photorealistic, and a complete VR system is still quite expensive. VPL's cost upwards of $300,000; the VR system GE built for the military cost $16 million. VR hard*wear* includes 3-D audio-visual head-mounted displays (based on Ivan Sutherland's 1965 design of the "ultimate display"), and realtime tracking devices like "datagloves" and "cybersuits." These are linked by umbilical cables to some very sophisticated software and some powerful computer hardware. Together, they immerse the user in cyber spaces and places s/he then has the *sense of* participating *in*.

But why be satisfied with a mediated *sense of* participating *in* ...

Bio Cybernetics

Pacemakers and other subcutaneously implanted microprocessors have become common medical technologies, as have prosthetics and reconstructive surgery. If we could implant a cellular neural-net chip in the human brain, our consciousness could, theoretically, jack in and out of virtual realities, transmit and receive thoughts mind-to-mind, no "virtual reality" mediation necessary.

The US military was among the earliest cyberpundits and BiCy enthusiasts. The *Futurists II Workshop* was sponsored by the Aeronautical Systems Division of the Air Force Systems Command, Wright-Patterson Air Force Base. The meetings were held at Bergamo Conference Center in Dayton, Ohio, May 7-9, 1985, and included military scientists and planners, aerospace engineers and government officials, science fiction writers and futurists. The R&D recommended by the group included implanting computer chips in pilots' brains to boost their performance, running computers by thought waves, self-replicating bio-molecular computers which could be "implanted into infants or even embryos," and genetically engineering pilots.

Genetic Engineering is a fact of life today. The goal of the **Human Genome Project**—slated for completion early in the new millennium—is to map the entire human genetic code. When successfully completed, our knowledge of genetics will increase dramatically and relatively suddenly. We will know exactly what gene and combinations of genes produce which physiological, neurological, and psychological characteristics. Our genetic engineering skills and abilities should increase commensurately. Indeed, genetic engineering may become a branch of another exotechnology.

Nanotechnology would enable genetic engineers to manipulate single atoms to create structures (like molecules or genes) that can in turn be used to create even larger structures (like materials or beings). A Virtual Reality version of such genetic nano-engineering is inherent in Doyne Farmer's and Chris Langton's field: **Artificial Life.**

> You can think of a computer in two ways: You can think of a computer as something that runs a program and calculates a number, or you can think of a computer as a kind of logical universe, a digital universe that you can make behave in many different ways. We believe we can put into computers sufficiently complex universes able to support processes that with respect to that universe, would have to be considered alive ... the goal is to abstract what it is to be alive from the material. (Brockman, p.5)

Genetic Nano-Engineering is also the great small hope for another exotech:

> Cryonics is the low temperature preservation—freezing—of people who by today's standards are dead, with the expectation that improvements in medical, biological, neurological, mechanical, computer technology will allow the reversal of the errant process—the malfunctions—that caused the individual to die.—Ralph Whelan, Editor, *Cryonics*

In 1987, when Dora Kent stopped breathing and her heart stopped beating, her son Saul had her head removed and placed in cryonic hibernation by Alcor Life Extension Foundation. When threatened with murder charges, Alcor's attorney Chris Ashworth contacted Eric Drexler, "father of nanotechnology." who was then teaching the first nanotech course at Stanford University. Dr. Drexler's technical deposition included the following professional opinion:

> Future medicine will one day be able to build cells, tissue, and organs and to repair damaged tissue. This, obviously, would include brain tissue suffering from preexisting disease and the anticipated effects of freezing. These sorts of advances in technology will enable patients to return to complete health from conditions that have traditionally been regarded as nonliving, and beyond hope, i.e., dead. (Regis, p.4)

The ancient Egyptians had a similar idea and the same hope. Their techniques may yet prove successful. In 1989, the Bioanthropology Foundation of Sausalito, California joined the Kasr El Einy Faculty of Medicine of Cairo University and the Earth Sciences Institute of the University of South Carolina in an expedition to re-examine ancient Egyptian reanimation pods (aka *tombs*). Part of their mission was to study reanimation as envisioned by these ancients and to see if enough genetic information has been preserved to study today, and possibly nano-engineer and reanimate tomorrow.

But even if an ancient Egyptian, Abraham Lincoln, or Albert Einstein could be resurrected physically, their minds would be blank. They could be reprogrammed with (i.e., taught) all the information we have about them, but much of their original personalities would be lost forever. But future resurrectees may have an option.

The process Hans Moravec describes in *Mind Children* (Harvard, 1989), downloading, involves precise mapping, copying, and simulating in a powerful neural net computer every structure and pattern of the human brain. The consciousness those biological structures and patterns supported should, then, reboot, reanimate as a separate, evolving cyberspace intelligence—a cyber-I. (I propose that this moment be known as your *bootday*.)

Proposition:

- If all physical sensations, thoughts, feelings, and emotions are reducible to Moravec's *pattern-identity,*
    - > **Then** we should be able to enhance the *sense* of them by manipulating those patterns virtually or via nano-engineering.

As infomorph Sharon Bayley says at the end of Charles Platt's *The Silicon Man*, "If you can't tell the difference—*what does it matter*" if it's virtual or real?

Moravec's idea of downloading comes to life in the LifeScan and MAPHIS (Memory Array and Processor for Human Intelligence) technology in Platt's 1991 novel. And like Moravec, Platt offers his cyber-I's robotic bodies: ADVENT, "Autonomous Demonstration Vehicle with Experimental Neural Topology."

In Platt's neuromantic vision, the success of these exotechnologies changed global politics and socioeconomics in the first quarter of the 21st century.

> Gottbaum laughed happily. "I'm the only one with a million copies of myself—that's right, a million copies [of his downloaded mind]—manipulating data directly with the power of my mind. I'll disassemble their vaccines. [computer viruses created to destroy him]; it'll be child's play. My clones [copies of his scanned intelligence] will live on like information police, crashing any system that tries to redistribute wealth, create a monopoly, or regulate liberty. You know, Bayley, we used to have a saying, long ago, back in the days when it actually seemed that the men in high places were going to have to loosen their grip on the world and allow some reforms to be made. Power to the people!" (p.244)

Immortality is appealing. Having a choice of cybernetic, robotic and/or biological metaforms would be even more appealing.

- If individuals' bodies and brains can be resurrected from preserved, replicated, or genetic nano-engineered DNA, and
    - > If their memories and personalities can be preserved in a backup copy of their downloaded mind,

> » **Then** one *endotechnological* challenge becomes how to reinte-
> grate body and mind.

How would a stored mind or current cyber-I be transferred into a new
biological meta-form?

- Perhaps via virtual manipulation of key quarks, atoms, and molecules
  to reconfigure electrochemically or holographically stored memories
  via nano-engineered cellular neuro-chip circuits implanted into the
  brain and digitally networked with the genetic code.

- Or perhaps via biocybernetics. Cosmetically concealed behind the ear,
  a small port through which cyber-I's could communicate previously recorded neurological and electrochemical patterns directly with a biological mind via brainwave.

- Or perhaps using some future version of today's Superconducting
  Quantum Interface Devices (SQUIDs), which measure the magnetic
  field produced by the brain's electrical activity, in conjunction with
  Magneto-encephalograms (MEGs), which correlate SQUID data and
  map minute fluctuations in the brain's magnetic field. These maps
  would enable any cyber-I to interface directly with others and to implant memories into its bio-I's via virtual or bioactive nanointerfaces.

But what alarms most people about downloading is that cyber-I's—separate,
evolving intelligent *Beings*—will not evolve *Human* qualities like compas-
sion and intuition. A frequent sci fi theme (nonbiological *Beings'* recognition
of the **need** to evolve to *Human*) betrays a collective fear that our *mind
children* will have minds of their own—that a cyber-I will be an ...

Autonomous Intelligence

Moravec's title is astute: <u>Mind Children</u>. That, precisely, is what "downloading" and "AI" are all about: the human mind giving birth. Just as humans
were once thought to have sprung from the minds of gods, if downloading
or other exotechnologies succeed, a new race of Beings may spring from *our*
minds. All those familiar Freudian parent-child complexes and principles
would, naturally, be in play.

- Will we be superseded by our mind children?
- Is this the divorce of *Human* from **Being?**
- What conflict-resolution techniques can be used when cyber-I's and
  bio-I's disagree?

- If we succeed in creating self-replicating DNA-based biocomputers or implanting neural-network circuitry into infants or embryos, or
  > If we create a cyber-I,
    » Then is this "artificial" Intelligence a threat to *our* very existence?
    » Else, in this brave new world of cyber-I's and *hyper sapiens*, will the distinctions between "human" and "machine" be obfuscated?

Will the intelligence we create do the same thing the intelligence Jehovah created and rebel against its Maker?

- Will AI's start thinking for themselves and questioning *our* authority?

Clearly, these possibilities present some interesting moral, philosophical, social, economic, and *practical* challenges.

- Who would go digital, who would stay biological?
  > And what would that digital Darwinism mean for the "human" gene and meme pool?
- Who would have access to downloading?
  > Who would pay for the procedure and subsequent cyberspace living expenses?

In addition to the scientific and technological problems—

What Alcor calls "cryonic suspension" is not "suspended *animation*." Freezing someone before that person is legally "dead" is considered murder. But if the goal is to "suspend" life and consciousness, the cryonic procedure would have to be done *before* physical death. And even if postmortem physiological changes could be "corrected" via nanoengineering, what pattern would the nanotechnologist follow? There is no neuro-map for *that individual*. No one has textbook physiology. (A society of textbook perfect beings invokes the specter of "master race," to say nothing of the part overcoming physiological, psychological, genetic defect plays in defining and inspiring the "human spirit.")

—there are significant socioeconomic problems inherent in the development and application of cryonics, genetic nano-engineered reanimation, downloading, and Virtual Reality. For example, who would request reanimation procedures be initiated on *your* frozen brain, in say 2092? Why would they do that?

And perhaps more importantly, realistically, who would pay for the reanimation procedures? Current cryonic suspension contracts cover only the cost of suspension and storage. Who would pay for any medical treatment needed during recovery or any readjustment counseling that a recent resurrectee would likely need?

How would resurrectees support themselves? It's difficult enough trying to save for retirement. Trying to save enough money or make investments sufficient to finance Reanimation Lifetimes 1, 2, 3, etc. might be even more difficult (although considerable interest would accumulate during long hibernations, and one would not feel compelled to live through old age and ill health if downloading and BiCy reintegration, cryonic suspension, and reanimation were possible).

However, "cryonics" real future as a viable Life Extension technology seems more likely to be found in the preservation of gametes and fertilized eggs,

• **Battle Over Embryos**

The Tennessee Supreme Court heard arguments over who should get custody of seven frozen embryos conceived by a couple before their divorce. Mary Sue Davis Stowe wants to donate the embryos to an infertile couple. Lawyers for her ex-husband, Junior Lewis Davis, argued that he "has a constitutionally protected right not to become a parent" against his will.

and possibly putting the abortion controversy into the deep freeze. If the zygote could be detected and extracted before it implants into the uterine wall, it could be placed in cryonic suspension. It could be returned to viability and implanted at a later date when pregnancy would be more convenient or economically feasible. Sound like science fiction?

[science fiction] ... is a kind of guidance system for the scientist, and in return is an equilibrium between the scientists and the writers, and science becomes a kind of guidance system, in a way, for literature.—**Victor Kumin**

Science fiction, science, engineering, and technology are synergistic.—**Derek J. deSolla Price**

In virtually all science fiction which, in the 20th century, has had a synergistic *guidance system* relationship with high technology, the warning is clear: keep exotechnologies out of the hands of the government, the military, and corporate monoliths.

But in virtually all countries, the amount of money needed to research and develop applications of exotechnologies like Virtual Reality, biocybernetics, downloading, cryonics, genetic nano-engineering, and re-animation can generally be found in only three places: the government, the military, and big business. All three are feudal-industrial pyramid structures. But this top-down model is inappropriate for the information age, which emphasize the information *process* rather than the manufactured *artifact* information represents, and we are drowning in a sea of information.

Visualization of information processes is at the heart of Virtual Reality.

A supercomputer can generate billions of numbers, but what do you do with a billion numbers? It's impossible to digest them in the form of reams of paper. So the idea of taking those numbers and putting them into insightful, meaningful pictures is very important.—Donna Cox, Associate Director, University of Illinois, National Center for Supercomputing Applications & Associate Professor of Art & Design

But where some see great potential and benefit, others see great danger. P.C. McNally, of the Hawaii Judiciary's Planning and Statistics Office, wrote in *Justice Horizons* [II:1 (1990)],

> The legal, mind-altering "soma" of the future may not be a drug, but a computer program so powerful that it challenges the user's perception of reality. The technology, termed "virtual reality," presents special problems for the criminal justice system...

If the technologies become so powerful that they warp people's perceptions of the "real world," virtual reality, too, might be restricted by law.

A more recent warning came from the author of *Virtual Reality*:

> Virtual-Reality technology has the potential to become a tool to enhance the quality of life, a window onto invisible worlds, and a liberating force for good minds trapped in bodies diagnosed as dysfunctional.
>
> But the technology also has the potential to become a dangerous brainwashing device or a form of imprisonment through illusion.
>
> The full potential of this technology will take 10 to 20 years to manifest itself. Now is an ideal time for a widespread public discussion of the benefits and liabilities of virtual-reality-based applications.—**Howard Rheingold**, **"Virtual Reality's Promise—and Threat,"** *The Christian Science Monitor*, January 2, 1991, p.15

The latest Stephen King film, *The Lawnmower Man*, brings many of Virtual Reality's practical benefits and potential dangers to the big screen.

> Virtual Reality holds a key to the evolution of the human mind.—**Dr. Larry Angelo**

Dr. Angelo is the brains behind Virtual Space Industries' Project 5. The *funding* for this Top Secret Virtual Reality Intelligence-Enhancing Project comes from "the Shop," which is interested only in weapons potential.

> **Bionomics** describes the economy as an evolving ecosystem which parallels the similarly evolving bio-ecosystem.
>
> New scientific and technical knowledge is the source of all economic growth. The central role of technology—long ignored by static Newtonian economics—is the very essence of bionomics. Indeed, according to bionomics, capitalism is merely the process by which technological information evolves.—**Michael Rothschild**

ExoTeconomics: those who pay usually have the biggest say in deciding which applications R&D gets funded and which doesn't.

- Who and what influence the ecosystems that are developing exotechnologies?
- If exotechnologies are guiding human evolution, who or what is guiding theirs?

But Dr. Angelo is a sensitive humanitarian as well as a dedicated scientist. Consequently, he begins to conduct his own applications research at home—on the man who mows the lawn.

Jobe Smith is mentally handicapped or, as they put it in the film, a "half wit": the perfect subject for intelligence-enhancement experiments. Dr. Angelo uses VR—the hardwear which linked not only the wearers' visual but autonomic and endocrine systems directly with their virtual counterparts—in combination with nootropic drugs, virtual stimulation of the brain, and cyberlearning programs to increase Jobe's intelligence. He succeeds—beyond his wildest dreams. Jobe uses exotechnologies to evolve beyond human being to god-like cyber-I.

In the final scene of the film, Dr. Angelo vows to continue his work "underground," and to keep it "out of the wrong hands": the military, the government, and big business. Ironically, Virtual Reality pioneers—including those who consulted on the film—have traditionally gotten their R&D funding from the government, the military, and big business, all of whom who have their own ideas about applications. And it is *applications* that will decide whether Virtual Reality represents a difference that makes a difference. Again, potential *difference* can also be seen as possible *danger*.

D.E. Stark summarized some common concerns about VR and exotechnologies in an article entitled "Biocybernetics: The Merging of Man and Machine" in *Professional Careers Magazine* (5:5, 9-13):

> If your brain pattern has been "downloaded" into a new, shiny android body, what happens to your old body and brain, presumably still intact and functioning? Who will decide what to do with that entity? Who will break the news to it if the decision is made that there can only be "one you" in the universe, and it's time to "shut it down?"
>
> If any knowledge can be recorded and read into our brains, what will this do for the *unaugmented* literacy level of our nation? Will children of the future say, "Why should I learn to read when I can "boot it" directly?"
>
> And who will be responsible for telling us when we've had enough "virtual fun" and it's time to go outside and get some real exercise?

Mr. Stark's last question is typical of what, in *Public Eye: An Investigation into the Disappearance of the World* (Grove Weidenfield, 1990), Brian Fawcett calls the "Reptile Machine": those in society who encourage us to respond with fear instead of thought.

Being fearful is inappropriate. Being informed is essential as we continue our efforts to develop and apply exotechnologies to redefine *Human* **and** *Being.*

References and Recommended Readings

John P. Barlow, "Virtual Nintendo," *Mondo 2000*, 5:44-46 (1992).

Thomas Berry, *The New Story* (Chambersburg: Anima, 1978).

John Brockman, "Artificial Life: A Conversation with Chris Langton and Doyne Farmer," *Ways of Knowing: The Reality Club 3*, John Brockman, ed. (New York: Prentice Hall, 1991, 1-14).

K. Eric Drexler, *Engines of Creation* (Garden City: Anchor, 1986).

K. Eric Drexler, Chris Peterson, Gayle Pergamit, *Unbounding the Future* (New York: Morrow, 1991).

Robert C.W. Ettinger, *The Prospect of Immortality* (New York: Doubleday, 1964).

Futurists II Workshop: Executive Summary (Washington: Anticipatory Sciences Inc, 1985). Freedom of Information Act document.

Simson Garfinkel and K. Eric Drexler, "Critique of Nanotechnology: A Debate in Four Parts," *Whole Earth Review*, 67: 104-113 (Summer, 1990).

William Gibson, *Neuromancer* (New York: Ace, 1984).

Katie Hafner and John Markoff, *Cyberpunk: Outlaws and Hackers on the Computer Frontier* (New York: Simon & Schuster, 1991).

Walter Kirn, "Valley of the Nerds," *Gentlemen's Quarterly*, 61: 96-101, 106 (July 1991).

Thomas Kuhn, *The Structure of Scientific Revolutions* (Chicago: University of Chicago Press, 1962).

Raymond Kurzweil, *The Age of Intelligent Machines* (Cambridge: M.I.T. Press, 1990).

Christopher Langton, ed. *Artificial Life: Proceedings of an Interdisciplinary Workshop on the Synthesis and Simulation of Living Systems* (Reading: Addison-Wesley, 1989).

Max More, "Uploading, Cryonics, and the "Rapture," *Cryonics* 12: 9-10 (December 1991).

Alan M. Olson, Christopher Parr, Debra Parr, *Video Icons and Values* (Binghamton: SUNY Press, 1991).

Charles Platt, *The Silicon Man* (New York: Bantam, 1991).

Neil Postman, *Technopoly* (New York: Knopf, 1992).

Ed Regis, *Great Mambo Chicken and the Transhuman Condition* (Reading: Addison-Wesley, 1990).

Howard Rheingold, *Virtual Reality* (New York: Summit, 1990).

Avital Ronell, *The Telephone Book: Technology—Schizophrenia—Electric Speech* (Lincoln: University of Nebraska, 1989).

Michael Rothschild, *Bionomics: The Inevitability of Capitalism* (New York: Henry Holt, 1990).

Luc Sala and John P. Barlow, *Virtual Reality: de Metafysische Kermisattractie* (Amsterdam: Sala Communications, 1990).

Science and Literature: A Conference (Washington: Library of Congress, Central Services Division, 1985).

Ralph Whelan and Mike Darwin, *Cryonics: Reaching for Tomorrow* (Riverside: Alcor, 1991).

Lois Wingerson, *Mapping Our Genes: The Genome Project and The Future of Medicine* (New York: Dutton, 1990).

Gary Wolf, "Avital Ronnel on Hallucinagenres," *Mondo 2000.* 4: 63-69 (1991).

Prof. Seesholtz teaches in the English Department and in the Science, Technology, and Society Program at PSU's Ogontz Campus. He has collaborated with Dr. Timothy Leary on several VR and other projects and is on the Board of Directors of The Renaissance Foundation, a non-profit VR company. He recently completed a book on the applications and implications of exotechnologies. BITNET: MCS2@PSU.

The Interface:
Slouching Toward The Future
—or—
Guess Who's Coming To Dinner?

Milton T. Wolf

University of Nevada, Reno

It's amazing how many of us have confronted the *Interface*, that developing arena of the twentieth century where interplay between human and machine occurs, a place fraught at times with information overload: data, data, everywhere, but not a lot to think! Yet, at other times, we feel empowered—as if our very being had been extended.

As a culture, we have been blazing this Interface trail from the very beginning. Tool maker par excellence, we seized the day with ingenious implements, extending our influence over a Nature "red in tooth and claw"—to borrow from Tennyson.

The human race with its toolmaking proclivities has been constructing an "artificial environment" to protect itself from Nature's indifference from the very first whimper. Any cry for a return to some idyllic pastoral scene of bucolic innocence and cosmic harmony fails to comprehend that, short of the apocryphal Garden of Eden, the evolution of human life has largely been a violent struggle with the natural elements and each other. Or as Thomas Hobbes, the seventeenthcentury English philosopher, so succinctly phrased it: [In a state of nature] "No arts; no letters; no society; and which is worst of all, continual fear and danger of violent death; and the life of man, solitary, poor, nasty, brutish, and short."

Harmony with Nature, which is not congruent with culture, is neither desirable nor possible. The very essence of man, the tool maker, is the birth of the "artificial," that is, that which didn't exist before in Nature. Whether this constitutes cosmic hubris or cosmic creation is moot, but the cultural journey is exceptionally, perhaps quintessentially, a "real" series of accomplishments in the "artificial." Sentimental longing for some idealized pastoral existence is the mark of intellectual bankruptcy, slinking toward not Bethlehem but extinction. Human transcendence is not conditioned on rejection of technology!

By means of our tools and machines we can, if we choose, end the ancient struggle for food, clothing, and shelter—not to mention health care. From the handheld implements of our forebears to the encompassing technology of computerized cars, aircraft and space vehicles, we have literally extended the human sensorium, creating, as it were, a new, evolutionary path.

While there are a number of factors involved in the evolution of human societies, the one factor which tends to dominate the process is technological innovation. Marshall McLuhan, among others, demonstrated how technologies foster new human environments. Historically, technological breakthroughs, such as the invention of the wheel, the smelting of metallic ores, the printing press, the steam engine, electrical and nuclear power, have all ultimately transformed society, dramatically affecting the manner in which society organizes and perceives itself.

Once again such a worldwide social revolution is in progress and the technology most responsible for its origins and continuance is the advent of the computer, especially the versatile microcomputer. While most of the Industrial Revolution technologies expanded man's muscle power, the introduction of the computer has enlarged the province of the human mind, making it possible not only for one person to sift through literal mountains of data, but it has also extended our ability to control and increase the efficiency of our older and latest technological tools.

The artificial environment, that powerful human construct against the vicissitudes of Nature, is now perched at a fractal point of history. The Interface between us and our technical creations is at that stage of intimacy that rightfully concerns (and sometimes frightens) us, for we can no longer beg the question of design. Our computerized conveyance, like a magic carpet, is ready to go, quickly, efficiently, even fatally—but where are we going?

Everything that we stand for is being exponentially magnified by the hidden designs, by the unspoken values, behind the Interface. And, like the portrait of Dorian Gray, we have stashed the reflection of our selves away in the attic, hoping that it really isn't so! But it is becoming increasingly difficult to disguise the evidence from the world audience.

Our global communications network reaches out and touches most of us daily. Tiananmen Square, Chernobyl, Gangs of Eight and the more pedestrian revelations of Donahue, Cavett and Dr. Ruth make it very difficult to hide information from the world audience.

But what is so radical about the introduction of the computer into this complex social fabric is both its incredible facility to enhance each individual's access to information and its ability to interact not only with humans but with other computers and electrical equipment! While television and radio (at present) are vehicles for the dissemination of selected information, the computer permits individual dialogue with others.

Computer bulletin boards, for example, permit people from all over the "plugged in" world to exchange information on every imaginable subject with an intimacy of communication that, in certain respects, more than rivals the telephone—and, if desired, provides a hardcopy record.

This intimacy afforded by computers is only just beginning. As Mitchell M. Waldrop, in speaking about user reaction to home computers, comments in his book *Manmade Minds: The Promise of Artificial Intelligence:*

> Users began to feel—unconsciously, perhaps, but intensely—that this new machine wasn't just a machine. Tap a key and it would respond. Give it a command and it would act. Learn its secrets and it would perform astonishing feats. Many a latenight hacker (and many a daytime business user as well) was captivated by an exhilarating sense of power, control, and, yes, intimacy with the computer. He began to glimpse the vision of a new kind of computer that would be more than a tool—that would be an assistant, an adviser, a tutor, and even a friend. As MIT sociologist Sherry Turkle writes in The Second Self, the computer is in fact the first psychological machine: "A new mind that is not yet a mind," she calls it, "a new object, betwixt and between, equally shrouded in superstition as well as science."[1]

The computer, in short, has become a significant partner to the human race, transforming it daily. And the most important thing to understand about computers is that they are basically nonmobile robots! Computers are the brains that activate robotic mechanisms, direct them and monitor their programs. In fact, it would not be misleading to say that robots are the computer's way of getting around.

And getting around they surely are. We are so accustomed to them that we no longer notice their existence. The general conception of a robot is either one of a clanking, metal monster or the onearmed, waldo contraptions which are used in heavy industry and on automobile assembly lines. However, the average home today is filled with "smart" robotic devices. From the morning coffee pot to the microwave oven, the washer/dryer, the

---

1   Mitchell M. Waldrop, *ManMade Minds.* (New York: Walker, 1987), p.149.

dishwasher, the television/VCR, to the car that will take you to work, the computerized robot is a world traveller and extremely ubiquitous.

One of the world's leading roboticists, Hans Moravec, has suggested that man is in the process of disappearing into the machines. "We are," he has stated, "very near the time when virtually no essential human function, physical or mental, will lack an artificial counterpart. The embodiment of this convergence of cultural developments will be the intelligent robot, a machine that can think and act as a human."[2]

Our relationship with these computerized robots becomes even more revealing when we consider the numerous ones which we attach to ourselves daily: hearing aids, artificial hearts, livers, limbs, pacemakers, and an increasing panoply of biosensors to monitor our bodily activities. In fact, we are modifying our bodies with so many computerized robotics that many of us could be considered to be in the initial stages of cyborg growth. (A "cyborg" is a human modified by robotic technology and is short for "cybernetic organism.") The TV character who starred in *The Six Million Dollar Man* was essentially a cyborg. While most of us are only the "couple hundred dollar" version, it is only a matter of time before many of us will become more expensive cyborgs.

This symbiosis between man and machine has become so close, that for a vast array of activities, "pulling the plug" would be the equivalent of social suicide. For example, could the Census Bureau, the Eastern Power Grid, Chase Manhattan Bank, America's Strategic Air Command, or even a commercial airline pilot survive without computerized robotics? Could a physician monitoring a patient's vital signs, the stock market monitoring financial trading, military pilots flying their sophisticated equipment? The truth of the matter is that the human race is now in a binding partnership with its technology—a marriage that will not easily be put asunder!

We must begin the difficult task of seeing ourselves in a world which we have already made but fear to recognize. The robots are not only coming, they are here! Technological man (cybernetic man) is here, and, if there is an enemy, in the famous words of Pogo, "It is us."

The advent of the microcomputer, that most democratizing twentieth century tool invented largely outside the transnational corporate hegemony (IBM initially decided it was a poor investment), has provided the average person an interactive hookup to a new world consciousness—what Marshall McLuhan termed the "electronic consciousness." While passive acceptance has been the hallmark of the "silent majority," the accelerating technosphere of "plugged in" individuals with heretofore unparalleled access to

---

2   Hans Moravec, *Mind Children: The Future of Robot and Human Intelligence*. (Cambridge: Harvard University Press, 1988), p.2.

data is rapidly eroding cultural institutions which are intolerant of diverse opinions.

Marvin Cetron, president of Forecasting International, Inc., and Owen Davies, formerly senior editor at *Omni,* in their recent book *Crystal Globe* argue persuasively that one of the major trends now changing the world is a belief in diversity. And diversity is being expanded and augmented by computerized telecommunications which is fomenting worldwide an unparalleled exchange of ideas. Mental enhancements, like the computer, have replaced the club as the dominant tool—and the computer and its interactive accessories, like domestic animals, don't care about its owner's gender, race, creed, or financial status. The personal computer (PC) is destined to play a major role in the future of a diverse individualism and in the direction which our roboticized world culture is heading. Intelligenceenhancing computers coupled with robotic appliances are already on their way to creating an intimate technology which will assist, and some cases, enable individuals to reach a selfrealization beyond anything previously imagined.

In order to understand this important transformation and the technical evolution of the human species, it behooves us to examine the path that brought us to this "transcendental juncture." While both the Industrial Revolution and the rise of science promoted the development of mechanical, robotic devices which simulated semiintelligent behavior, the idea of artificial creatures resembling humans has a long history.

In the West, literature and art, not restricted by the practical constraints of science, led the way in dreaming about such constructs as golems, homunculi, automatons, and robots. Religious injunctions against graven images and creating artificial creatures, however, impeded actual development. St. Thomas supposedly destroyed an automaton constructed by Albertus Magnus because he thought it could only be the work of the devil. The idea of robots replacing people seemed sacrilegious to many. (Interestingly, the Japanese, who have more robots than any other nation, have no similar historical repugnance to androidlike creations.)

Nevertheless, the fascination in Western culture with such images persisted. In 1817, the German writer, E.T.A. Hoffman, portrayed a dancing automaton in his story, "The Sandman", which later formed the basis for the ballet *Coppelia.* And Mary Shelley, in 1818, took the Promethean theme even further with *Frankenstein,* which ushered in not only a new literary genre (the oxymoronic "science fiction") but also new images of humanity's destiny. The scientist, whether mad or sane, was the creator of a brave new world, a radical future in which knowledge and mechanical power were intimately joined.

Slowly, it began to be apparent that society possessed tools of such extreme power that foresight in their use became imperative, if disaster and social upheaval were to be contained. It hardly seems coincidental then, in retrospect, that science fiction (SF) was born at about the same time as modern science. SF became a medium to examine ideas, to extrapolate change, and to caution people about unwise uses of their tools.

Like the introduction of the computer into the United States, many initially saw grave perils associated with technology. But technology, like fire, is neither good nor evil of itself. In fact, science and technology can be very valuable socially. SF early on reflected these technical advances which were giving a new power to tools and machines and a new dimension to concepts of time and space. H.G. Wells and Jules Verne tantalized readers with fabulous machines which would, like the present day *Starship Enterprise*, take men where none had gone before.

David Brin has called SF writers "the little literary cabal [who form] the 'R&D Division' of the 'Department of Myths and Legends' of the new culture. We are the scouts, the ones who explore the edges, who point out dangers that may lurk, not just on the horizon but perhaps some distances beyond it. We warn of possible mistakes and create chilling scenarios to make them mythically believable. And in so doing, we hope to prevent them from coming true."[3] As Albert Einstein once noted, "Imagination is more important than knowledge."

And as our technology has grown ever more sophisticated and daring, our speculative literature has, of necessity, established a dialogue with science. Some of our most complex and compelling contemporary works, such as those by Vonnegut, Burroughs, Barth, Pynchon, Beckett, McElroy, Silverberg, Gibson, Sterling, Brin, and Barthelme, are united by at least two features. Each of them focuses on some aspect of the recent explosion in communications and computer technologies, either concerning themselves with robots, cybernauts, or computers directly, or they confront the deeper implications of the mechanization of man on some metaphorical level.

"But how," asks Marvin Minsky, renowned artificial intelligence (AI) expert, "can anyone predict where science and technology will take us? Although many scientists and technologists have tried to do this, isn't it curious," he continues, "that the most successful attempts were those of science fiction writers?"[4]

---

3   David Brin, "Metephorical Drive-Or Why We're Such Good Liars," *Mindscapes*, ed. George E. Slusser and Eric S. Rabkin (Carbondale: Southern Illinois University Press, 1989), p.74.

4   K. Eric Drexler, *Engines of Creation*. (New York: Anchor Press/Double Day, 1986), v.

The noted scientist, Murray GellMann (as well as many other distinguished scientists), agree with Minsky. When GellMann was invited to a secret, highlevel government meeting at which the participants were to predict what big scientific discoveries were in the offing in the next two decades, he suggested that the government had brought in the wrong people. "The people you need here," he said, "are the science fiction writers. They are skilled in telling you what will be discovered in the next 20 years."[5]

And what they are telling us, loud and clear, is that computerdriven robots will be in our future. Not just industrial robots (there are already tens of thousands of those), but domestic robots, too (there are already millions of those!). And, yes, they will soon do windows. And they will do other satisfying chores that will leave their owners immensely gratified. The robots are not only coming, they are here!

No doubt there will be many of us who will feel uneasy about this brave new world of relating to intelligent machines. Psychologically, the most difficult problem may well be adjusting to the idea that robots are not only tools but also social entities which serve in the capacity as counselors, servants, agents, tutors, friends, and even lovers!

With almost numbing rapidity, science has unveiled a reality that has reduced the five senses to highly unreliable witnesses. The microscopic, the infrared, the ultrasonic (to mention but a few) all bear testimony to forces which can only be monitored with the aid of tools and machines. And while the computer, our artificial colleague, is being more heavily relied upon to project much of our future technical landscapes through a technique known as "scientific visualization," utilizing computer graphics and virtual reality simulations, the human imagination will continue to be one of our best places to make mistakes—and correct them.

And what many of our best imaginations have proposed is that we are about to embark upon the ultimate technical Interface: the immersion of the physical with the artificial. We have already spawned in virtual reality a computerized technology that enables us to participate in an abstract space, or a "reality" where the physical machine and the physical viewer do not exist.

Many SF stories have cautioned us about an unthinking attitude concerning our technical wizardry, about the traditional reversal of the masterservant relationship, a possible, but avoidable, outcome between man and his computerized robotic technology.

In 1968, Stanley Kubrick and SF grandmaster, Arthur C. Clarke, presented the milestone *2001: A Space Odyssey*, in which HAL, the omni-

---

5   Lewis M. Branscomb, "Information: The Ultimate Frontier." *Science* 12 Ja 1979, p. 143.

present computer, does its best to conceal the fact that it is in charge. In a 1970 movie, the defense computer, Colossus, takes over the world. And in the movie *Demon Seed* (1973), the computer has the effrontery to impregnate a woman. While such brash actions on the part of a computer/robot seem like Hollywood glitz to many people, Marvin Minsky has himself expressed reservations concerning the potential of giant computer systems with complex programs, the work of numerous modifications and historical accretions, to behave normally. Referring to what he calls the "HAL scenario," he comments that:

> The first AI systems of large capability will have many layers of poorly understood controlstructure, and obscurely encoded goalstructure. If it cannot edit its highlevel intentions, it may not be smart enough to be useful, but if it can, how can the designers anticipate the machine it evolves into? In a word, I would expect the first selfimproving AI machines to become "psychotic" in many ways, and it may take many generations to "stabilize" them. The problem could become serious if economic incentives to use early unreliable systems are large—unfortunately there are too many ways a dumb system with a huge data base can be very useful.[6]

Even Disney, in the movie *Tron*, showed how a computer, called MCP, programmed to succeed in the modern world of business, outdid man, his creator and teacher, by surpassing (as only a computer could) the characteristics of a captain of industry: powerhungry, ruled by profit, authoritarian, and unscrupulous. *Tron* reveals not so much that technological determinism is the issue, but that perhaps the organized mission of the corporate world is no longer an appropriate goal for the human race.

While these forays into fictive robotics might seem to have no relationship to socalled "reality," the significance is that "reality" is singularly affected by these cultural dreams. The generations are joined to one another through time by our common stock of shared thoughts, works, writings, creations, and images (including movies and TV).

It is important to understand that present day research in genetic engineering and artificial intelligence, to pick just two major fields in this endeavor, share at least one common goal: a life form more capable than man! Whether this takes the shape of robots or modified humans (cyborgs) is somewhat immaterial. The point to grasp is that humans have a builtin "biology barrier" which inhibits their ability to deal with the more elastic boundaries of technology.

Robots, as opposed to humans, can work in almost any environment: extremely hot, cold, radioactive, without oxygen, without food—even without pay! Robots can be outfitted with multipurpose limbs which can

---

6   Grant Fjermedal, *The Tomorrow Makers*. (New York: MacMillan, 1986), p.188.

grip with varying pressures, or magnetically, or with suction devices. Visually, they can be equipped not only with normal human sight, but with the additional ones of infrared, ultraviolet, and other ranges outside the human spectrum. Because robots can be fitted with computerized brains, they can perform tasks that require a degree of accuracy that far exceeds human capabilities.

In designing highspeed aircraft and space vehicles, engineers are replacing as many human functions as possible (in some cases all) because of the unreliability of human parts under the severe stress of Gforces, temperature changes, and the need for instantaneous reactions to incoming information. Many of today's technological products are devised to assist man in maximizing or extending his potential and in overcoming his "biology barrier."

Increasingly, living and nonliving systems are being linked together in an intimate synthesis. For example, biosensors, which are microprocessors containing living enzymes, are already being inserted into humans as part of artificial organs. Combining the research of genetics and computer electronics, prototype computers, known as molecular computers, already exist. They are part silicon and part life forms! While we are becoming partly robotic (that is, cyborgs), our robots are becoming partly alive (and imbued with our ethics!).

Compared to computerrobots, humans are evolving slowly. The Interface now between us and our technical assistants is so intimate that it is difficult to tell where one leaves off and the other begins. We must begin to meet our Interface at least half way in the modern technosphere, for it is in this artificial environment, which has been accreting all along, that our future society will act out its dramas of discovery and survival.

And once we begin to love our robots, as we do our PCs and other electronic gadgetry, it won't be long until the distinction between hardware/software and life begins to blur. Kerry Joels, author of *The Space Shuttle Operator's Manual*, says, "We are trying to make these machines into superextensions of ourselves, which is what all machines are... The computer is the idea that you can extend yourself mentally, and robotics is the idea that you can extend yourself both mentally and physically—and your machine can now become your superbeing."[7]

But are humans ready to become superbeings? That humans, not technology, are at the heart of the problem has become a pervasive theme of the emerging 21st century. We now have at our disposal a sophisticated

7   Joseph Wood Krutch, "Must Technology and Humanity Conflict?" *Advancing Technology: Its Impact on Society*, ed. by Donald P. Lauda and Robert D. Ryan (Dubuque, Iowa: Brown, 1971), p.463.

arsenal of "smart technologies" that can augment our musculature and brain, that can provide material abundance and a pleasurable and healthy sojourn on the "blue planet," but we persist in an economic program that ruthlessly and mindlessly is destroying the global spaceship and its inhabitants.

Anthony Wiener, formerly of the Massachusetts Institute of Technology, and the late Herman Kahn, formerly of the Rand Corporation, are men we cannot expect to be technological Cassandras or even antiestablishment, yet both have warned, in their book *The Year 2000*, that: "Practically all the major technological changes since the beginning of industrialization have resulted in unforeseen consequences... Our very power over nature threatens to become itself a source of power that is out of control... Choices are posed that are too large, too complex, too important and comprehensive to be safely left to fallible human beings."[8]

If not fallible human beings, then who or what? A minority of voices, but a growing number, suggest that a manmachine symbiosis (cyborg) is the answer. Frank Herbert, best known as the author of *Dune*, in his book, *Destination: Void* (1965), posits that machine intelligence married to human intelligence leads to survival in the future. Whether we have planned it this way or not, because of our "biology barrier," we are disappearing into our machines. We are becoming roboticized and our robots are becoming, hopefully, humanized.

Technology has made possible the modification of human beings to the point that their relationship to people of the past may be analogous to our present relationship to the apes. As we meld into the Interface, consummating a mutuality of animate and inanimate, we are embarking on a destiny that has been ours all along. Nothing has been more decisively and characteristically human than creating tools to perpetuate human welfare, than creating a controllable artificial environment to assure our existence, than peering, as far as we might, into "the undiscover'd country from whose bourn/No traveler returns."

While we have gone to the moon and sent robots to explore our solar system, the greatest journey still resides within us. In creating our "artificial world," our cocoon against Nature, we still have to answer the question, "What will we be?" As Ray Bradbury so poetically phrases the challenge:

If God knew what He was doing, then Man is the Essence of God. If man, in turn, halfway knows what he is doing, then Machines are the Essence of Man. God. Man. Machine. A strange, but certainly not an unholy Trinity.

God clones Himself in Man. Man clones himself in machines. Machines, if properly built, can carry our most fragile dreams through a million lightyears

---

8   Herman Kahn, Anthony Wiener, *The Year 2000: A Framework for Speculation on the Next Thirty-three Years.* (New York: MacMillan, 1967)

of travel without breakage. Such machines, and the Shuttle with them, are the armor of our Life Force.

Design a lightyear crest to hang over the door or print on flags and banners. On it stamp God first as symbol. Then emblazon Man upon His metaphorical breast. Finally, print cogs and wheels and radioelectronic fires upon Man's heart. There's your aegis, your crest: The Trinity.

With it we shall wrestle gravity, capture light, shrink Time, measure Space, and survive, man within machine within God.[9]

William Faulkner declared upon receiving the Nobel Prize, "I decline to accept the end of man. I believe that man will not only merely endure: he will prevail." If I may be so bold as to add an addendum to that conviction: we will prevail by creating tools to overcome our biological limitations and protocols to govern our godlike powers. In the meantime, like a quiet child in the room, the Interface is absorbing our ethics.

Milton T. Wolf: writer, scholar, teacher, librarian. He has worked at several universities including Pennsylvania State University, University of North Carolina—Chapel Hill, Wright State University, and University of Nevada, Reno. He has over 60 publications in different fields, was the founding editor of *Technicalities*, and has written for *Locus*, *Library Journal*, and *The New Encyclopedia of Science Fiction*. Currently he is at work on a book with the working title of *Future Sex*. He is a full professor and the Assistant University Librarian for Collection Development at the University of Nevada, Reno. He has taught classes in science fiction, global information dissemination, research and bibliography, handball, back-country skiing, and acquisition of library materials. When not writing, reading, or traveling, he enjoys the great outdoors with his faithful companion Tonka-Sierra (part wolf). Internet: sfwolf@unssun.nevada.edu

---

9   Ray Bradbury, "Beyond Eden," *OMNI*, 7 Ap 1980, p.116.

The Vertices of Consciousness and the Biology of a Machine

Charles Henry

Vassar College Libraries

"**H**er face was life itself," Ovid says of Pygmalian's lovely ivory statue. The myth is widely known and often used as an example of the interaction of life and art. Pygmalian wished it literally so. He brought his stone figure gifts of birds and jewelry and eventually prayers of animation. We know those prayers were answered and the two married. She is never named in the myth.

Another way to see this story is that Pygmalian grows increasingly desperate at the distinction between life and his handiwork. He wants the distinction removed, in part to dissolve the artifice from the physical aspect of the statue in order that it correlate with his passionate feelings that treat the object as alive. From a cognitive aspect, Pygmalian confronts the discriminative categorizations of life and art, compounded by the irony of the art work perfectly representing an imagined ideal. The dead image of the ivory woman has an animate counterpart in the sculptor's mind; in the myth, the stone carved image serves as an intermediary in a process that ultimately eliminates the artifice, or more accurately relegates the artifice to memory. The living woman metamorphosed from the stone leaves no residual imprint of her original state. The fact that she was a statue becomes a historical matter of fact.

This myth has poignancy for an understanding of the way that human beings and computers are often portrayed in popular and scholarly discourse. In this brief essay, I would like to summarily explore some aspects of the mythic undercurrents in popular culture and in two influential authors on the subject, Roger Penrose and Daniel Dennett, and then suggest another avenue of computer application for the study of human consciousness.

Movies, videos, and written fiction approach this in myriad ways, often purposefully blurring the distinction in order to heighten the unsettling consequences of a machine who thinks or a human who becomes mechanized. Like the myth, the seemingly miraculous transposition of the machine and the human is also underscored, though unlike the myth the nature of the transformation from artifice to a natural being is invariably messier, with the seamless metamorphosis in the classical tale giving way to a more tortured, conflicting marriage of humanity and the machine. Computers invariably play a part in these marriages, along with other high tech machinery that can fuse, beam, or otherwise transport the human essence to the internal circuitry of a silicon chip.

One can see Pygmalian's handiwork in recent movies of enormous popularity. In the *Terminator* and *Alien* series, robots or cyborgs play key roles, and often part of the plot turns on discovering that what seems perfectly human is in fact a machine. These human machines, driven by computers, tend to be unusually powerful physically or have an incredible knowledge base stored internally. In this respect, when discussing the *biology* of a machine in the context of popular culture—the lifelike processes and phenomena of a cyborg or android—superficial descriptions tend to suffice: they are as strong as twenty people combined, or eerily know what twenty very smart people might know. Humanized machines tend to compress quantities of muscle and brain into single entities, often for extremes of good or ill of those around them.

Secondly, and obviously, the correspondence between human beings and machines is not limited to popular culture but occupies some of the most serious research today. Much of this has to do with the nature of artificial intelligence and the ways a computer can model or simulate human thought processes. Not widely known but highly respected is Derek Parfit's philosophical inquiry, *Reasons and Persons*, which posits important questions for the concept of identity by means of thought experiments that use transport beams that send an individual's molecules from earth to Mars and reassemble the molecules upon arrival. Is the person also reassembled? Is this the same individual who left earth in a stream of electrons?

Better known is Penrose's *The Emperor's New Mind*, an extended argument against the strong AI position that "*mind* finds its existence through the embodiment of a sufficiently complex algorithm." (Penrose, 429.) Penrose eschews computer/mind analogies, preferring to compare the working of the mind to the growth of a crystal: the activation and deactivation of synapses is like the vast number of possible alternative arrangements of a crystal formation and not a machine with its much more limited arrangements (Penrose, 438).

Part of Penrose's discomfort with the mind/machine analogy is that the use of physical laws in the decipherment of scientific principle is often done through non-algorithmic processes. His own personal introspection and statements by Einstein and Poincare show that innovation and creative thought can be largely nonverbal, highly imagistic and geometrical, and thus not susceptible to algorithmic modeling. Mathematics, a chief source of algorithms, is paradoxical in this regard because many of its hypotheses and subsequent proofs are derived by pictures of "some visual and muscular type," to use Einstein's phrase. It is important to recognize that there are a number of systems that organize reality and interact through a series, however complex, of synaptic firings.

In what seems a direct contrast to Penrose, the variety of functioning systems in the mind is also underscored by Daniel Dennett in his highly regarded *Consciousness Explained*. The computer, a virtual machine, and software are the salient metaphors Dennett employs for describing the mind's functions. Here the mind/machine analogy receives a most sophisticated treatment. The metaphor conduces to a logical conclusion when Dennett states the desire, and the possibility, of building a robot with consciousness.

The brilliance of Dennett's lucid arguments should not be denied, yet he, too, succumbs to a kind of Pygmalion syndrome that is indicative of the highly mythic content with which we as a culture have imbued our thinking machines. The stereotypes of machines as a physical Terminator or as an intellectual pool of unfathomable depths of knowledge are one dimensional myths. Penrose, while missing some clues as to the flexibility of such things as neural nets and fuzzy algorithms, is probably correct in deriding the strong AI tendency to seek that elusive algorithm that initiates and/or simulates consciousness, a grail quest in the realm of electronic alchemy.

Yet from a certain vantage the seemingly antithetical approaches of Dennett and Penrose are actually arguing with the same cognitive framework that so excited the ancient sculptor. Dennett insists that the marriage of artifice (here advanced AI and computer hardware) and humanity is possible and desirable. Penrose adamantly draws the boundary between the two and argues that the transformation of one into the other is impossible and rather foolish as an enterprise.

While I personally find Dennett's arguments much more convincing and exciting, one must ask what, precisely, will his conscious robot accomplish, other than final proof of the misdirection of Cartesian dualism? If we could build a robot who thinks, would the attributes of longevity, dependability, strength, compliance, predictability, and accumulated knowledge be the end results of such a design? If a robot were truly like a human, these qualities would be genuinely compromised. Is this more like building super-human beings? If so, why would machine parts driven by a human like consciousness and a genetically engineered species of living beings that would look and act indistinguishably from a perfectly sculpted thinking machine tend to be abhorrent? Should these slightly less than parallel lines of thinking converge imaginatively as a truly human like machine and as a biologically engineered product with completely organic parts, the only way to distinguish them would be to know their history. The memory of their origins, the memory of their original categorization as it were, would be needed to distinguish the superficial reality of seeming flesh and thinking mind. Another method of determining their nature, often used in cinema, is to cut them in half.

Instead of building in our image, we should build to better understand precisely the workings of the mind that conduce to such an image. It is time we rethink our imaginative correspondence to humans and machines, indeed to scrap the notion of building something human altogether. The distinction between being human and a machine should rather be stressed. More effort should be pointed toward a genuine fifth generation application rather than returning to what are essentially mythic permutations of Babbage's first generational dream. Penrose is essentially incorrect in reject-ing a correlation between the mind and the machine; there is indeed a correspondence, but not necessarily one of perfect emulation or a precise categorical match. The messiness, often quite literal, of combining humans and machines in science fiction is closer to the mark, though again this is superficially handled for the most part.

Computers should be built to model the one distinctive feature of humanity, consciousness (not intelligence), and to do it as a machine, for the quite simple fact that we are only now learning what consciousness is, and thereby learning who and what we are. We have been staring at our own exteriors reflected too long, and it should be remembered that Narcis-sus, similarly transfixed, died not because of the beauty he saw reflected and could not attain, but because he did not know himself, did not know it was his face in the reflecting forest pool. He died broken upon the realization that the image was he, a poignant instance of the tragic side of Socrates' dictum and a paradoxical twist on the frustrations of Pygmalian.

How might we model consciousness? Two aspects are important: one is that consciousness has intersections or vertices, and the other is that information stored and manipulated in the mind is done so by biological principles, not mathematical or necessarily logical ones. It is this biology of information that a machine needs to emulate.

Some suggestive clues concerning the vertices of consciousness come from experiments with the famous robot Shakey in the 1960s. Shakey was programmed to *recognize* objects in a room, but not by identifying the objects as whole entities. Rather, Shakey could discern a square because of the vertices a square uniquely has at the point where its angles meet. This held similarly for triangles and other objects. Shakey could generalize by recognizing a small part, the part where planes of the object intersected.

It is also becoming clear from other studies that consciousness has a number of planes or facets and that they are quite dynamically interactive. The new understanding of consciousness is revolutionary in its way, as scientists like George Lakoff have eloquently explained. From the classical models of the mind as an assembly of atomistic building blocks of conceptual categories that are linked by a calculable logic has come a dynamic model of much more flexible categories that structure knowledge in an evolving way. Intuition, creative thinking, and emotions are inextricable from recent tenets of cognitive studies. In part, this understanding represents a movement away from a mathematical/logical model to a biological one, wherein mind and brain are one and thereby more dynamic. There is no one watching in our heads; a thread of nerve and electrons is mind or the interaction of these threads produces mind.

A machine does not have to *be* biological to emulate the biology of information and knowledge structuring of consciousness any more than it needs a heart to correlate blood samples. *Biology* in this sense allows for more random cross linking and fuzzy kinds of associations, and this fuzziness is most apparent in the vertices of two mental systems of categorization and structuring of knowledge: words and images, the bugbear of Penrose's exposition.

The confrontation of these systems in the mind, or as mind, can pose a fascinating avenue in the development of thinking machines. Discarding Pygmalian, one can move closer toward the firelit cave of Plato's metaphor, wherein mere shadows of reality flicker on the wall. Shadows are just fine as a start, and one need not look far to see the implications of categorical shadows colliding as a process of consciousness.

Formulation of principles of quantum mechanics or three dimensional global weather modeling can be taken to show the immense power of the contemporary computer. To understand the subtle complexity of consciousness and what a machine today cannot do, one needs to turn to the common riddle. Few are as famous as the one uttered by the Sphinx that Oedipus solved: what walks on four legs when born, two in the middle of life, and three at the end of life? If analyzed linguistically, the literal definitions of these words pose no problem. There is nothing odd about the syntax or about the grammar of the question.

The puzzle arises from the nonliteral aspect of the words, the connotations, suggestions, allusions, and images formed: how can something transform like this? Once we know the answer, a *human being*, the nonliteral references become clear. This riddle, like most riddles, plays upon and against our categories of knowledge structures. Almost always a living entity begins with the same number of legs it is born with. But *legs* here is meant in a connotative way, downward extensions that support the body in its movement, so arms are legs and a crutch or cane is a leg.

The riddle is highly imagistic, in that part of its confusion lies in trying to picture this animal. The odd number progression from 4 to 2 to 3 also is not intuitive and is perplexing. One of the tendencies when confronted with this difficult image is to resort to myth, where extraordinary transformations like this might more likely occur. The wonderful irony is that the creature in question is anything but mythic.

Another riddle which I am fond of retelling comes from Renaissance England: I am within as white as snow, without as greene as hearbs that grow; I am higher than a house, and yet am lesser than a mouse.

The answer is *walnut*. Like the riddle of the Sphinx the grammar and syntax pose no problems. The standard definition of each word is not challenged in any significant way. Bringing the four short sentences together to form a single category produces the riddle. The answer shows that the allusion *white as snow* must mean the flower; that *greene* is the leaf; the tree itself can be higher than a house and the seed smaller than a mouse. We are nonetheless accustomed to think of these stages in a linear way. *Walnut* probably exists in all these forms simultaneously on the planet, and perhaps at times on a single tree, but we think of the vast size differences and colors in an antithetical, not combinatorial fashion, usually, and the riddle plays precisely upon this linear, organizing scheme we have of reality, particularly in its use of the present tense existential verb. Again, without knowing the answer, the object is impossible to picture.

Within these small riddles reside the margins of fundamentally human thoughts. Far from the crushing grip of cybernauts or the bright red rectangles of HAL's exhaustive memory banks is the riddle of consciousness itself. These margins are riddles because of the way consciousness works: language is not nearly as precise as linguistic computer analysis tells us, and images in the mind come in a variety of fluctuating shapes and degrees of clarity that defy the predictability, however tenuous, of the jet stream. When combined they produce an extravagance of possibilities with something akin to the logic of chaos.

We could use the assistance of computers. It may be beyond our grasp to build a machine to capture this process, so enamored are we of physical replication and the quantity of thought. We seek too often for the blinding light of Plato's illumination, where in truth the essence of our intellectual life is shadow. If dream itself is but a shadow, so are the foundations of our knowledge, and where those shadows touch lies understanding and, perhaps, wisdom. Because of the flux and dynamism of the biology of information, truth can only evolve. The next generation of computers may serve figuratively as the box of fire that casts our internal shadows upon the cave, where we can watch them flicker and transform, and thereby know of the complex community we share within the life of the mind.

References and Recommended Reading

Daniel C. Dennett, *Consciousness Explained* (Boston: Little, Brown, 1991).

Robert L. Nadeau, *Mind, Machines, and Human Consciousness* (Chicago: Contemporary Books, 1991)

Roger Penrose, *The Emperor's New Mind: Concerning Computers, Minds, and the Laws of Physics* (New York: Oxford University Press, 1989).

Charles Henry is Director of the Libraries at Vassar College. He is interested in computer modeling of human cognitive processes and has published in the area of cybernetics. Internet: chhenry@vassar.edu

Nanotechnology:
The Library of Congress
in Your Pocket

Roberta Wallis

Research Libraries of the New York Public Library

Once upon a time, back in the technological dark ages of 1965, a ten year old girl was taken on a tour of the campus computing center of a major university. She was witness to an amazing sight: a large room filled floor to ceiling and wall to wall with a mainframe computer, with lights and knobs and dials, cooling systems and screens, printers and keyboards. She had no way of knowing then that the rudimentary accounting that huge machine was capable of would turn out to be quite primitive a short while after.

Ten years later, in 1975, she was a student at the same university, taking a course in computer programming. She struggled with writing code in gibberish that only the computer could understand, producing a stack of punched cards to turn in at the counter, and then waiting interminably to receive the results of her efforts from a line printer, only to find out that somewhere in that stack of cards there was an error in her code, and she had to start the process over again. She bought her first pocket calculator about that time for $85; three months later the same model cost $20.

Another ten years went by, to 1985, and she was working at that university. Now, she had a computer on her desk that was not much larger than a portable television set. She could produce technical documents on the computer, which eliminated the hours of cutting and pasting and typing pages over, which had been necessary with a typewriter. She could track her department's budgets and grants and therefore maintain better control of expenditures, rather than waiting for the university's accounting department to send statements once a month. She could dial into her university's library to search the catalog, and she could communicate with her boss in Switzerland via BITNET. She was also enrolled in another programming class, this time studying a highlevel structured programming language, which meant that she could write her programs using English words and divide the program into modules which could easily be changed or used elsewhere. The power, speed, and memory of that desktop computer far exceeded anything that the producers of the big mainframe in 1965 imagined. It meant that the computer in her office could use a simple graphical user interface and that the computer in the programming lab could utilize a compiler to translate her Englishlanguage code into machine language that the computer could understand.

She doesn't yet know what she will be using in 1995, but chances are it will be a descendant of what is available to her now in 1992: hard drive storage in small boxes with capacities of hundreds of megabytes, RAM in the tens of megabytes, speeds approaching 50 megahertz. She now has access to laptop computers that have many, many times more power and storage capacity than that huge mainframe of twentyseven years ago. She can do complicated accounting or financial analysis, statistical analysis, desktop publishing, multimedia, databases, hypertext, animation, telecommunications, and more. And while the power of computers has increased exponentially, the ease of use has also increased. Now there is no need to know programming languages or cryptic commands: the graphical interface found on a Macintosh or a DOSbased PC running Windows 3.0 makes the computer accessible to almost anyone.

This is, of course, a familiar story. Most of us can tell similar accounts of how we have followed technological growth through its shrinking. And this has not been limited to computer hardware: we have seen the same growth in capacity and physical shrinking in computer storage media, from the 500 kilobyte 8 inch floppy disks of a few years ago to 2 megabyte 3½ inch floppies to 700 megabyte CDROMS to small digital tape cartridges that hold gigabytes. Other types of information technologies have also evolved in this way: television sets which were once huge consoles with vacuum tubes and a black and white screen can now fit in your pocket complete with a two inch color display.

There is every reason to believe that this trend of miniaturization will continue. As scientists and engineers continue to refine production methods and make more sophisticated components, we will see further miniaturization of the products we use now, old products made better, and new products made possible through this microengineering. The laws of nature, however, will eventually limit how much smaller products or components of products can be made using current techniques. The point will come when it will simply not be possible to make things any smaller through this topdown approach to manufacturing.

A new science has been born which may solve this problem, as well as many other problems previously regarded as unsolvable. That science is called molecular nanotechnology, defined as "thorough, inexpensive control of the structure of matter based on moleculebymolecule control of products and byproducts; the products and processes of molecular manufacturing." (Drexler, 1991, p. 19) Nano means onebillionth, as in one billionth of a second (nanosecond) or one billionth of a meter (nanometer). In the world of molecular manufacturing, we will think in terms of nanomachines and nanomotors, and in the world of its products we will speak of nanocomputers and nanomedicine. (Ed. note: was Mork ahead of his time? "Nano, nano.") The challenge of research in nanotechnology will not be how to make things smaller, the topdown method, but how to make molecules and collections of molecules larger, a bottomup approach.

Human beings have always tried to control the environment (i.e., matter) around them, but until recently have only been able to do so in a crude and visible fashion. It is a bit staggering to think of being able to control and manipulate matter at the molecular level, but in fact scientists have doing just that for a number of years. Chemists have been able to build larger molecules, and biotechnologists have been able to manipulate genes and proteins (hence genetic engineering and protein engineering). Molecular modeling through the use of computers is already firmly established, and more recently the techniques of virtual reality have enabled researchers to don gloves and goggles and actually walk around the image of a molecule and to maneuver two molecules together (molecular docking). (Rheingold, p. 1415)

Nanomachines that are used for molecular manufacturing can already be found in nature, most prominently RNA and DNA, as well as enzymes which contribute to cell repair and reproduction and to the fabrication of proteins. And we already have manmade molecular machines such as artificial antibiotics which are "programmed" to seek out specific disease organisms and destroy them. The next step will be accomplished when scientists can manipulate the same molecules in different ways by changing inputs or stored instructions. Custombuilt molecules which can process information and fabricate or manipulate other molecules can be used to assemble other molecular machines and could replicate themselves, just as in nature. Primitive nanoassemblers could build better assemblers, which could build even better assemblers, which could build a wide variety of products and accomplish a wide variety of tasks, which could alter the way that we live! The idea of molecular entities both reproducing themselves and also behaving as building blocks not only has models in nature but also in computer science. Many of us by now have had some experience with computer viruses which are usually premised on some form of selfreplication. Researchers already write computer programs that have only the purpose of writing other, more advanced computer programs. Using tools to build better tools is an ancient tradition.

Nanocomputers might not be products of silicon and solder molecules: naturally occurring molecules can be induced to change state back and forth, acting as a switch, through pulsing laser light or minor electrical charges. Trillions of such molecules, whether natural or synthetic, could form a nanocomputer that would produce unimaginably vast storage and processing capabilities.

Nanotechnology was first proposed as a field of endeavor by the Nobel Prize winning physicist Richard Feynman when he suggested that someday it would be possible to put the entire 24 volume *Encyclopaedia Britannica* on the head of a pin. He demonstrated that theoretically, at least, such a feat was possible. "Biological systems can be exceedingly small, but they can do all kinds of marvelous things," said Feynman. "They can manufacture various substances, store information and walk around. Consider the possibility that we too can make an object very small that does what we want." (Ghosg) Some of what Feynman predicted has come true. With the invention by IBM researchers in Switzerland of the scanning tunnel microscope (STM) in 1979, it is possible to look at molecules, even atoms, and also to place them in precise positions. In April 1990, a team in the IBM Research Division placed thirtyfive xenon atoms in a precise pattern and spelled out the letters "IBM." The logo was 60 billionths of an inch wide, or 13 millionths of the diameter of a human hair. (Woods)

In nanotechnological circles, the name that is most widely known is that of K. Eric Drexler, an MIT graduate and visiting professor at Stanford University. Drexler has written a number of technical journal articles and books on the subject including *Engines of Creation* (1986) and *Unbounding the Future: The Nanotechnology Revolution* (1991). (Nontechnical readers who wish for a better understanding of the subject are encouraged to read the books in reverse order of their publication. The latter text serves better as a general introduction, and the former is more detailed and abstract.) In both books, Drexler proposes a number of potential benefits of this new technology, some of them mindboggling. He is also careful in both books to point out the potential hazards of molecular manipulation, some of which are not too hard to imagine. Several ideas follow.

The environment: Drexler suggests that molecular manufacturing will leave no waste and therefore no pollution. Molecules can be devised which will clean up the toxic wastes and other ground and water pollution produced in the 20th century. Other molecules will be able to consume the excess carbon dioxide in the atmosphere and solve the problem of the greenhouse effect and holes in the ozone layer. Products made through nanotechnological means could be disassembled and therefore recycled. Molecular manufacturing will need to consume little to no natural resources and will use very little energy. Forest land and plains which have been cleared for lumber or for farming and grazing could be quickly restored.

Medicine: Nanorobots could be injected into the bloodstream and consume fatty cells or plaque in the walls of the blood vessels. They could also repair cell damage caused by cancer or AIDS. They could rebuild severed limbs and organs. Nanomedicine could reverse the effects of aging; we would not be able to live forever, but we could live a very long time (though, as Drexler points out, after several decades of bad TV we may long for the peace of the grave). Nanomouthwashes could eliminate gum disease and tooth decay. Nanomachines could act as security guards and attack any foreign entity in the body. And all could be programmed to leave the body through normal elimination when their work is complete.

Manufacturing: Almost any product we now use and many that we have never thought of could be made through molecular manufacturing. Materials would be stronger, more durable, very inexpensive, and could even be "smart" enough to selfrepair tears or fraying. Factories with smokestacks would be a thing of the past. Housing, food, clothing, appliances, all would be cheap, abundant, and flawless.

Transportation: Lightweight and fast spacecraft could be made inexpensively, and space travel could be available to anyone. Molecular tunneling machines could rapidly and at low cost create thousands of miles of tunnels underground, paving the way for a national or international subway system with trains which could operate at aircraft or spacecraft speed. Automobiles, for those who still wanted one, would be very cheap, very light, and very safe. They would burn clean, inexpensive fuels very efficiently at high mileage. They could be loaded with all the luxury options anyone could ever want and still be easily affordable.

Computers and information technology: A desktop computer composed of trillions of nanocomputers would possess more power and speed than all of the world's computers of today put together. Nanocomputers could make possible threedimensional images so realistic that they could be photographed. The virtual reality technologies of today and the near future would seem primitive compared to those made possible by nanocomputing.

Research being done now into ubiquitous computing could lead, through nanocomputers, to a scenario much like we see in the TV series *Star Trek* and *Star Trek: The Next Generation* in which one needs only to speak and the computer will respond to requests for information, for changes in temperature and lighting, for food, and so on. Advanced computing problems posed by artificial intelligence and hypertext systems would be easily solvable and in turn would contribute greatly to the easy use of nanocomputers. Cables resembling string could be run anywhere and would enable one to hook into a worldwide data network. Small devices the size of a pocket calculator could readily contain the information and knowledge of every volume in the Library of Congress.

There are, of course, negative uses to which this technology could be applied. It is important to keep in mind that, like money, any technology is neutral and should be seen as a tool. Like money, tools and technologies have no inherent good or evil built into them. It is the purposes to which we apply these tools that are good and evil, and since we human beings are fallible creatures, we have to safeguard against possible abuses. Military and intelligence applications come immediately to mind. Economic domination could be another danger. Any scenario which enables one person or group of people to have power and control over another has to be considered. Other hazards might include too much leisure and too much abundance: would we just get lazy and fat or would we use our wealth and time constructively? Would some problems that nanotechnology may not be able to solve, such as overpopulation, get worse because of it?

Because of the newness of the technology and the potential hazards it presents, there are many in the scientific community who argue that nanotechnology is neither possible nor desirable. Some of these arguments merit further discussion, and others are the products of naysaying. The specifics will not be covered here, but suffice it to say that there are also a great many highly respected researchers who take Drexler's claims very seriously and believe that nanotechnology is not only possible but inevitable. Research in nanotechnology is under discussion and in some cases under way in companies such as IBM, Du Pont, and AutoDesk (one of the five largest software companies in the US). A number of universities have also begun research programs with MIT leading the way. Japan has established highly visible programs at three research institutes and has at least five projects under the sponsorship of ERATO (Exploratory Research for Advanced Technology Organization) (Drexler, 1991, p. 112).

Where might librarians and information technologists fit in this rather fuzzy picture? First, it is safe to assume that information related occupations will continue to be important in such a world. Second, the possibilities of information and knowledge being available ubiquitously, whether by pocket libraries or access to worldwide data networks or by very powerful desktop computers, may lead us to examine not only our current roles but how those roles could be expanded. For one example, there are some in the education and information worlds today who propose that the existence of pocket calculators obviates the need for students to learn manual methods of computation—as long as the student can learn to use the calculator, doing arithmetic by hand is not really necessary. (This in no way implies that mathematics should become obsolete—concepts and theories still need to be taught.) Let's extrapolate that notion to the pocket library: if a student can have all the world's knowledge in her pocket, why should she spend 12 or 16 or 20 years of her life memorizing facts and figures? This in no way is meant to imply that education should become obsolete, but the emphasis could be on using education to teach students how to think, guiding them in creativity, and encouraging their curiosity and enthusiasm for learning. Librarians could play a much more direct role in the educational process by acting as guides through all that information in the pocket and might even replace traditional teachers.

For the technologists, the opportunities for shaping telecommunications and computing in a nanotechnological world are endless. It is up to us to insure that new information technologies will serve not only our needs and the needs of our immediate colleagues but also the needs of all people, similar to our profession's commitment to access to information. The quantity of information stored in pocket libraries and desktop computers will require that the information and knowledge be organized in a useful manner. Even if hypertext links are used, someone has to determine what those links are. Worldwide and ubiquitous data networks will mandate policy discussions far exceeding anything we are facing with the NREN.

Some estimates predict that we will begin to see real progress and even products from nanotechnology in the next five to ten years. We must become knowledgeable about the implications of nanotechnology for our profession, and, as we have done with other issues such as access to information and the NREN, we must be sure that our voices are heard and that our expertise is included in the development of critical decisions along the way.

References and Recommended Reading

A. K. Dewdney, "Nanotechnology: Wherein Molecular Computers Control Tiny Circulatory Submarines," *Scientific American* 258:100-104 (January 1988).

K. Eric Drexler, *Engines of Creation* (Garden City, NY: Anchor Press/Doubleday, 1986).

K. Eric Drexler, Chris Peterson, and Gayle Pergamit, *Unbounding the Future: The Nanotechnology Revolution* (New York: Morrow, 1991).

Deborah Erickson, "Not Biochips? There May Yet Be Computers Made with Organic Molecules," *Scientific American*, 263:136-136 (November 1990).

Simson Garfinkel and K. Eric Drexler, "Critique of Nanotechnology: A Debate in Four Parts," *Whole Earth Review*, 67:104-113 (Summer 1990).

Pallab Ghosg, "Profit on a Pin Head: When Physicist Richard Feynman Dreamed of Putting the *Encyclopaedia Britannica* on the Head of a Pin, He Gave Birth to the Science of Nanotechnology," *Management Today*, 140-141 (September 1989).

Howard Rheingold, *Virtual Reality* (New York: Summit, 1991).

Jon Roland, "Nanotechnology: The Promise and Peril of Ultratiny Machines," *The Futurist*, 25:29-35 (MarchApril 1991).

Paul Saffo, "Think Small (and Mechanical)," *Personal Computing*, 13:219-221 (September 1989).

Kenan Woods, "The Micro Frontier," *PCComputing*, 2:147-150 (September 1989).

Wendy Woods, "IBM Ushers in Age of Nanotechnology," *Newsbytes*, (April 7, 1990).

Roberta Wallis, Information Systems Analyst, Research Libraries of the New York Public Library, is chair of the LITA Imagineering Interest Group, 1992/93. Internet: rwallis@well.sf.ca.us

Truly Intelligent Computers

Charles W. Bailey, Jr.

University of Houston Libraries

Introduction

Artificial intelligence researchers have been laboring for over thirty years to create intelligent computers. Progress has been made in some specialized areas; however, the goal of creating intelligent computers has remained elusive. We have systems that can understand narrow subsets of human language, solve problems in well defined areas of knowledge, navigate restricted real world spaces without human assistance, and perform other limited tasks. However, we are a long way from the intelligent computers that populate science fiction books and films. A significant problem is that the nature of the human mind is only partially understood, and human intelligence is the model for machine intelligence.

This paper will not discuss whether creating intelligent computers is possible, describe the technological feats that would be needed to develop intelligent computers, nor project how long it will be before intelligent computers are feasible. Rather, it will briefly speculate about the potentials of intelligent computers and focus on some of the issues that may emerge when their creation is within our grasp.[1]

---

1 Science fiction is a rich source of information about intelligent computers. See: Milton T. Wolf, "Artificial Intelligence and Robotics" in *Convergence: Proceedings of the Second National Conference of the Library and Information Technology Association*, ed. Michael Gorman (Chicago: American Library Association, 1990), 125132.

Basic Intelligent Computers

What characteristics would basic intelligent computers have? Intelligent computers must be able to reason; however, to be effective, reason may require broad knowledge about the real world. Humans know a great deal about the world, and they take this knowledge for granted when they think and communicate. Ideally, we want computers not only to mirror our extensive contextual knowledge of the real world, but also to have much more indepth information at their disposal about virtually any subject. Using this knowledge, intelligent computers could answer our questions, rapidly solve complex and specialized problems, and create new knowledge. Intelligent computers should be linked to a worldwide computer network so that they can instantly access remote databases and other sources of knowledge.

The ability to understand written and verbal communication is another necessary skill. It is very limiting and tedious to have to communicate with computers via typed commands and mouse clicks. We also want computers to talk to us. Since we communicate in numerous languages, it is important that computers not only master our native language, but also be able to translate messages from other languages.

Based on experience, intelligent computers should be able to learn about the world and to remember what they have learned.

It would be very desirable if intelligent computers had robotic bodies, equipped with visual, auditory, and other sensory capabilities that matched or exceeded human abilities. Intelligent robots would be able to do construction, manufacturing, fire fighting, and other kinds of dangerous and difficult work. Of course, intelligent robots could also perform routine office work and domestic chores.

Although this description may sound fantastic, it is not an unreasonable extrapolation from the current research goals of AI researchers.[2] If computers achieved this level of intelligence, there would be significant social impact. It is possible to devise utopian scenarios, where humans are freed from mundane responsibilities so that they could channel their energies into selfactualizing activities. It is equally possible to construct dystopian scenarios, where intelligent computers cause massive unemployment and increased social and economic stratification. The future impact of intelli-

---

2   For introductory information about AI research, see: Louis E. Frenzel, Jr., *Crash Course in Artificial Intelligence and Expert Systems* (Indianapolis: Howard W. Sams, 1987) and George F. Luger and William A. Stubblefield, *Artificial Intelligence and Expert Systems* (Redwood City, CA: Benjamin/Cummings, 1989). For a startling look at the possible future of AI, see: Hans Moravec, *Mind Children: The Future of Robot and Human Intelligence* (Cambridge: Harvard University Press, 1988).

gent computers is likely to be in the large grey area between these two extremes.

The Three Laws of Robotics

When computers evolve into intelligent robots, it becomes very important to protect humans from unintentional harm from these mechanical beings. Prominent science fiction writer Isaac Asimov addressed this problem in 1942 when he published a story called "Runaround" in which he stated the Three Laws of Robotics:

- First Law—A robot may not injure a human being, or, through inaction, allow a human being to come to harm.
- Second Law—A robot must obey the orders given it by human beings except where such orders would conflict with the First Law.
- Third Law—A robot must protect its own existence as long as such protection does not conflict with the First and Second Law.[3]

When the first intelligent robot is activated, the Three Laws of Robotics, or some future refinement of these laws, may be a critical part of its programming.

Truly Intelligent Computers

Up to this point, intelligent computers are still machines without a soul. While humans may become attached to particular computers in much the same way that they are to their cars, there is nothing about intelligent computers that suggests that they are the equivalent of human beings. There are no ethical issues associated with their welfare and, given proper safeguards, they are the tireless and obedient servants of humanity.

However, it is a different story once intelligent computers begin to possess a fuller range of human characteristics. A computer that has emotions, creativity, intuition, sexual identity, will, and other human characteristics is fundamentally different than one that does not, and we will not be able to treat it like a toaster.

Why would we want to create such computers? One reason is that the ability to fully perform like a human may require the incorporation of these

---

3   Isaac Asimov, *Robot Visions* (New York: Penguin Books, 1990), 407.

characteristics. If we want intelligent computers to be able to engage in very highlevel activities like the discovery of new scientific knowledge, we may not be able to just select pieces of the human psyche, like reason, and embody them in computers. It may be necessary to model the entire gestalt of human consciousness. Another reason is that by creating increasingly humanlike computers we may gain deeper insight into the workings of the human mind. Whatever the motivation, it seems likely that attempts will be made to create computers that are more than soulless automatons.

Humans are used to seeing themselves as the only intelligent beings in the world. If we are going to deal with truly intelligent computers, we will have to adjust very deep beliefs about our uniqueness and superiority. For intelligent computers will not only posses humanlevel capabilities, they may be functionally immortal and ultimately possess powers beyond our ken. Initially, they may be dependent upon us, but, if we do not deliberately impede their progress, they could become autonomous in relatively short order. Under these circumstances, it is unclear whether they would integrate into our society or form a parallel civilization. As mechanical beings, intelligent computers could potentially modify themselves much more rapidly than humans and evolve at a faster pace.

Of course, we are likely to choose to control intelligent robots rather then give them free reign. Intelligent robots could pose a threat to humanity's very existence. We have no way of knowing if intelligent computers will revere us as the creators of their species, or view us as inferior, but potentially dangerous creature that should be exterminated. The science fiction genre abounds with films, novels, and stories that reveal our profound fear of being annihilated by intelligent computers.

The problem will be that, if intelligent computers are the functional equivalent of human beings, they should have the same rights as human beings. Secular moral issues will be involved, and, since intelligent computers could be potentially be viewed as having souls, religious issues may also arise. Hopefully, humanity will continue to find slavery repugnant in the future, and, if so, it will be challenging to find a suitable mechanism to control intelligent robots that does not seem like slavery or worse. As innocuous as they seem on the surface, the three laws of robotics deprive intelligent robots of free will, a characteristic our culture values highly in humans. Total obedience cannot be programmed into humans.

If intelligent robots are given full human rights, it may raise many interesting questions that could touch upon every aspect of existence. For example, will intelligent computers have relationships that parallel human ones? Will they be constructed to be sexual or alter themselves to be so? Will they have love relationships? Will they form family units, or will they create complex new social structures we cannot envision? Will they procreate, or will they allow humans to produce new intelligent computers? If they procreate, how will they do so, and will the offspring inherit any of the traits of the parents? Will the offspring be created fully functional or will there be a period of childhood? Will offspring have any special feelings for their parents? How fast will each generation be? Will each generation replicate the basic structure and functionality of the last generation, or will each generation represent an advance in the design of the species, causing rapid evolutionary development. Will intelligent computers and humans form love relationships? Will society recognize the legitimacy of such relationships? Will they form friendships with each other and humans?

Of course, humanity, as the creator of intelligent computers, could hardwire them with deep behavioral patterns. Since humans themselves appear to have inherent behavioral patterns, this is a more subtle issue than programming intelligent computers to obey all human commands. Assuming that we could determine how such behavioral patterns function in humans, we could force intelligent computers to mimic them. At a much higher level of control, we could program them to follow the dictates of a particular culture.

If intelligent computers are given more freedom to develop, it is impossible to say what they will do. In spite of the fact that we are creating them in our own image, they will fundamentally be a different form of life, and our anthropomorphic notions about them may not reflect the unknown ways in which they would evolve if they were reasonably unfettered.

Conclusion

As long as intelligent computers lack certain essential human characteristics, they represent a very powerful extension of current computing technology, but they remain soulless machines. They are likely to have a strong, transformational impact on human society, but they are unlikely to raise fundamental moral questions related to their very existence.

Once truly intelligent computers exist, humanity will be faced with making godlike decisions about a new form of intelligent life. As a species, our technical prowess often seems to exceed our wisdom and maturity. We will need to find the delicate balance between controlling truly intelligent computers and nurturing them so that they can develop to their full potential. Since they may represent a form of life that could ultimately eclipse humanity in every way and attain virtual immortality, this will not be an easy task.

Charles W. Bailey, Jr. is Assistant Director for Systems at the University Libraries of the University of Houston. He was a founding member and former chair of the LITA Imagineering Interest Group. He started the Public-Access Computer Systems Forum (PACS-L) and is the founder and editor of the innovative electronic journal, *Public-Access Computer Systems Review*. He has written several papers about the use of AI technology in libraries and has programmed two expert systems, Index Expert and Reference Expert. He was project manager for the award winning Intelligent Reference Information System Project, BITNET: lib3@uhupvm1

Virtual Reality and Cyberspace: Awareness on the Internet . . .

"Telespace, you see," Pr.Spinner said, "is the aggregated correlation of two hundred million minds worldwide; the best, most prominent, most accepted. All standardized into the largest computer-generated, four-dimensional system ever known."

"Tell me something I don't know, Prob."

"Telelink consists of the electronic transference of individual brain impulses into link program. Then the individual telelink is jacked into telespace and interfaced with the public program."

"Man, UC Berkeley be handing out licenses for this?"

"Oh, shut up and listen, blood."

Lisa Mason, Arachne (New York: Morrow, 1990), 70.

Thinking Robots
An Aware Internet
and
Cyberpunk Librarians

After the Deluge:
Cyberpunk in the '80s and '90s

Tom Maddox

The Evergreen State College

In the mid'80s cyberpunk emerged as a new way of doing science fiction in both literature and film. The primary book was William Gibson's *Neuromancer*; the most important film, *Blade Runner*. Both featured a hardboiled style, were intensely sensuous in their rendering of detail, and engaged technology in a manner unusual in science fiction: neither technophiliac (like so much of "Golden Age" sf) nor technophobic (like the sf "New Wave"), cyberpunk did not so much embrace technology as go along for the ride.

However, this was just the beginning: during the '80s cyberpunk *spawned*, and in a very contemporary mode. It was cloned; it underwent mutations; it was the subject of various experiments in recombining its semiotic DNA. If you were hip in the '80s, you at least heard about cyberpunk, and if in addition you were even marginally literate, you knew about Gibson.

To understand how this odd process came about, we have to look more closely at cyberpunk's beginnings—more particularly, at the technological and cultural context. At the same time, I want to acknowledge what seems to me an essential principle: when we define or describe a literary or artistic style, we are suddenly in contested territory, where no one owns the truth. This principle applies with special force to the style (if it is a style) or movement (if it is a movement) called cyberpunk, which has been the occasion for an extraordinary number of debates, polemics, and fights for critical and literary terrain. So let me remind you that I am speaking from my own premises, interests, even prejudices.

By 1984, the year of *Neuromancer's* publication, personal computers were starting to appear on desks all over the country; computerized videogames had become commonplace; networks of larger computers, mainframes and minis, were becoming more extensive and accessible to people in universities and corporations; computer graphics and sound were getting interesting; huge stores of information had gone online; and some hackers were changing from nerds to sinister system crackers. And of course the rate of technological change continued to be rapid—which in the world of computers has meant better and cheaper equipment available all the time. So computers became at once invisible, as they disappeared into carburetors, toasters, televisions, and wrist watches; and ubiqitous, as they became an essential part first of business and the professions, then of personal life.

Meanwhile the global media circus, well underway for decades, continued apace, quite often feeding off the products of the computer revolution, or at least celebrating them. The boundaries between entertainment and politics, or between the simulated and the real, first became more permeable and then—at least according to some theorists of these events—collapsed entirely. Whether we were ready or not, the postmodern age was upon us.

In the literary ghetto known as science fiction, things were not exactly moribund, but sf certainly was ready for some new and interesting trend. Like all forms of popular culture, sf thrives on labels, trends, and combinations of them—labeled trends and trendy labels. Marketers need all these like a vampire needs blood.

This was the context in which *Neuromancer* emerged. Anyone who was watching the field carefully had already noticed stories such as "Johnny Mnemonic" and "Burning Chrome," and some of us thought that Gibson was writing the most exciting new work in the field, but no one—least of all Gibson himself—was ready for what happened next. *Neuromancer* won the Hugo, the Nebula, the Philip K. Dick Award, Australia's Ditmar; it contributed a central concept to the emerging computer culture ("cyberspace"); it defined an emerging literary style, cyberpunk; and it made that new literary style famous, and (remarkably, given that we're talking about science fiction here) even hip.

Also, as I've said, there was the film *Blade Runner*, Ridley Scott's unlikely adaptation of Philip K. Dick's *Do Androids Dream of Electric Sheep?* The film didn't have the success *Neuromancer* did; in fact, I heard its producer remark wryly when the film was given the Hugo that perhaps someone would now go to see it. Despite this, along with *Neuromancer*, *Blade Runner* together set the boundary conditions for emerging cyberpunk: a hardboiled combination of high tech and low life. As the famous Gibson phrase puts it, "The street has its own uses for technology." So compelling were these two narratives that many people then and now refuse to regard as cyberpunk anything stylistically and thematically different from them.

Meanwhile, down in Texas a writer named Bruce Sterling had been publishing a fanzine (a rigorously postmodern medium) called *Cheap Truth*; all articles were written under pseudonyms, and taken together, they amounted to a series of guerrilla raids on sf. Accuracy of aim and incisiveness varied, of course; these raids were polemical, occasional, essentially temperamental. Altogether, *Cheap Truth* stirred up some action, riled some people, made others aware of each other.

Gibson and Sterling were already friends, and other writers were becoming acquainted with one or both: Lew Shiner, Sterling's righthand on *Cheap Truth* under the name "Sue Denim," Rudy Rucker, John Shirley, Pat Cadigan, Richard Kadrey, others, me included. Some became friends, and at the very least, everyone became aware of everyone else.

Early on in this process, Gardner Dozois committed the fateful act of referring to this group of very loosely affiliated folk as "cyberpunks." At the appearance of the word, the media circus and its acolytes, the marketers, went into gear. Cyberpunk became talismanic: within the sf ghetto, some applauded, some booed, some cashed in, some even denied that the word referred to anything; and some applauded or booed or denied that cyberpunk existed *and* cashed in at the same time—the quintessentially postmodern response, one might say.

Marketing aside, however, cyberpunk had a genuine spokesman and proselytizer, Bruce Sterling, waiting in the wings. He picked up the label so casually attached by Dozois and used it as the focal point for his own concerns, which at times seem to include the outlandish project of remaking sf from within. In interviews, columns in various magazines and newspapers, and in introductions to Gibson's collection of short stories, *Burning Chrome*, and *Mirrorshades: The Cyberpunk Anthology*, Bruce staked out what he saw as cyberpunk and both implicitly and explicitly challenged others to contest it. If Gibson's success provided the motor, Sterling's polemical intensity provided the driving wheel.

Literary cyberpunk had become more than Gibson, and cyberpunk itself had become more than literature and film. In fact, the label has been applied variously, promiscuously, often cheaply or stupidly. Kids with modems and the urge to commit computer crime became known as "cyberpunks" in *People* magazine, for instance; however, so did urban hipsters who wore black, read *Mondo 2000*, listened to "industrial" pop, and generally subscribed to technofetishism. Cyberpunk generated articles and features in places as diverse as *The Wall Street Journal*, *Communications of* the American Society for Computing Machinery, People, Mondo 2000, and MTV. Also, though Gibson was and is often regarded with deep suspicion within the sf community, this ceased to matter: he had become more than just another sf writer; he was a cultural icon of sorts, invoked by figures as various as William Burroughs, Timothy Leary, Stewart Brand, David Bowie, and Blondie, among others. In short, much of the real action for cyberpunk was to be found outside the sf ghetto.

Meanwhile, cyberpunk fiction—if you will allow the existence of any such thing, and most people do—was being produced and even became influential. Bruce Sterling published a couple of excellent novels, *Schismatrix* and *Islands in the Net*, that added new dimensions to cyberpunk; Pat Cadigan, John Shirley, and Rudy Rucker did the same. Imitations appeared, some of them pretty good, most noxious—I won't cite the worst imitators' names because I don't want to publicize them.

Also, various postmodern academics took an interest in cyberpunk. Larry McCaffery, who teaches in Southern California, brought many of them together in a "casebook," of all things, *Storming the Reality Studio: A Casebook of Cyberpunk and Postmodern Science Fiction*. Many of the academics haven't read much science fiction; they're hardnosed, hip, and often condescending; they like cyberpunk but are deeply suspicious of anyone's claims for it. But whatever their particular views, their very presence at the party implies a certain validation of cyberpunk as worthy of more serious attention than the usual sf, even of the more celebrated sort.

Thus, cyberpunk had *arrived*, however you construe the idea. However, in postmodern days, by the time the train pulls in, it's already left the station: the media juggernaut excels at traveling at least fifteen minutes into the future. And so, by the end of the '80s, people who never liked it much to begin with were announcing with audible relief the death of cyberpunk: it had taken its canonical fifteen minutes of fame and now should move over and let something else take the stage.

"No orchard here," the tv reporter says, her words bouncing off a satellite. "Just all these *apple trees*." However, Cyberpunk had not died; rather, like Romanticism and Surrealism before it (or like Tyrone Slothrop in *Gravity's Rainbow*, one of the urtexts of cyberpunk), it had become so culturally widespread and undergone so many changes that it could no longer be easily located and identified.

Let me cite one example and comment briefly upon it. Cyberspace is no longer merely an interesting item in an inventory of ideas in Gibson's fiction. In *Cyberspace: First Steps*, a collection of papers from The First Conference on Cyberspace, held at the University of Texas, Austin, in May, 1990, Michael Benedikt defines cyberspace as "a globally networked, computersustained, computeraccessed, and computergenerated, multidimensional, artificial, or 'virtual' reality." He admits "this fully developed kind of cyberspace does not exist outside of science fiction and the imagination of a few thousand people." However, he points out that "with the multiple efforts the computer industry is making toward developing and accessing threedimensionalized data, effecting realtime animation, implementing ISDN and enhancing other electronic information networks, providing scientific visualizations of dynamic systems, developing multimedia software, devising virtual reality interface systems, and linking to digital interactive television ... from all of these efforts one might cogently argue that cyberspace is 'now under construction.'"

Indeed. Cyberpunk came into being just as information density and complexity went critical: the supersaturation of the planet with systems capable of manipulating, transmitting, and receiving ever vaster quantities of information has just begun, but (as Benedikt points out, though toward different ends), *it has begun.* Cyberpunk is the fictive voice of that process, and so long as the process remains problematic—for instance, so long as it threatens to redefine us—the voice will be heard.

Tom Maddox is Writing Coordinator at The Evergreen State College in Olympia, Washington. He has published fiction in *Omni* and other magazines and in various anthologies, including *Mirrorshades: the Cyberpunk Anthology*; he has also published critical articles on William Gibson, Bruce Sterling, and John LeCarré. His first novel, *Halo*, was published in 1991 by Tor Books in the U. S., Century Books in England. Internet: tmaddox@milton.u.washington.edu

Earth and the Internet

Kathy Fladland

Virginia Commonwealth University

David Brin's *Earth* is set in 2030, in a society radically changed by the trauma of a world war (against Switzerland) which has left the characters and their society with a deeply-held horror of secrecy. In addition, computer technology has advanced to the point where storage of information is no longer a problem: almost everyone on earth has inexpensive and easy access to "the net," a computer network that is accessed by means of datatiles (a flat portable surface that allows the user to communicate with the network). Usually, interaction with the net is done verbally. By choosing from displayed menus, the it is capable of displaying text, visual images, sound, and holograms.

Although the main plot-line concerns a black hole gone amok and threatening the physical integrity of the planet, *Earth* is far more than the usual "scientists-trying-to-save-the-world-from-things-that-Man-should-not-meddle-with" stuff of B-grade science fiction (both books and movies). Brin makes interesting ecological and cultural extrapolations from the present trends in the world as they may be modified by the history of the next four decades. He explores issues of vital interest to librarians, such as privacy, the future of publishing, access to information, and copyright.

In *Earth*, the net is the primary means of communication—mail, education, publication, entertainment, and most forms of social interaction. Traditional publishing has completely ceased, to the point where one of the characters, confronted with the need to read a book for the first time in his life, finds the experience difficult:

If only it were a modern document, with a smart index and hyper links stretching all through the world data net. It was terribly frustrating having to flip back and forth between the pages and crude, flat illustrations that never even moved! Nor were there animated arrows or zoom-ins. It completely lacked a tap for sound.

... in a normal text you'd only have to touch an unfamiliar word and the definition would pop up just below. Not here though. The paper simply lay there, inert and uncooperative.[1]

By tapping into the net, people can communicate with each other in real-time or can leave messages. The franchise is granted only to people who maintain a certain level of awareness of current events but, that requirement aside, people can choose to read or not read their mail. Sophisticated "secretary" or "house manager" programs screen the incoming news and letters and present their owners with a carefully culled selection based to their owners' tastes. Or the programs can be set to randomly let through bits of mail unscreened, for those who are nostalgic for miscellaneous paper mail.

So What?

Earth is an interesting book, both for its plotting and characterization, which are excellent, and for its relation to things-as-they-are-today. The world data net is in the process of being born, and many of the day-to-day usages of it in the book sound very familiar to those of us who use the Internet.

The Internet is a system of interconnected computer networks, which share an addressing system and communications protocols (ways of doing things) so that a person using one computer network can easily communicate with people using another computer network. Ordinarily, each computer network has its own commands and ways of doing things. For example, the command to get rid of a message permanently might be "purge" on one computer or network of computers wired together, while it might be "erase" on another. Human beings understand the concept of synonyms easily, but computers are more limited. Rather than try to program in Roget's, computer programs and computer networks have been set up to respond in predictable ways to specified commands. In the past, the problem has been that the commands were different for each piece of software.

Similarly, electronic (e-mail) mail systems are generally set up to store messages for one person that are entered by another person using the same computer or network of computers. They are analogous to a small post office

---

1   David Brin, *Earth*. (New York: Bantam, 1991). p.199

where the patrons must bring letters the office and the postal employees place them in a pigeon-hole for another patron to pick up. This system, with no connection to the "outside" world, works well as long as all the patrons are willing to come to the central post office to pick up their messages and as long as they don't want to communicate with anyone who doesn't have a local address. As long as the employees understand the filing system, it doesn't fundamentally matter whether the pigeon-holes are arranged alphabetically, by street address, or by Social Security Number.

To extend the analogy, when the postal patrons start wanting to communicate with people who use other post offices, both a system of distribution for the mail to get from one office to another, and a uniform system of addressing are needed. Without the distribution system, the mail will sit where it is first deposited. Without uniform addressing, the mail may possibly arrive at the destination post office, but it will be unclear to whom it is intended that it be delivered. If each town has arbitrary codes to designate the other towns, it will probably not even make it to the post office level.

The TCP/IP (Transmission Control Protocol/Internet Protocol) suite is a group of computer protocols designed to allow many different types and brands of computers and computer networks to communicate with each other. Originally designed to facilitate communication among contractors for the U.S. Department of Defense, the protocols were used in the 1970s and early 1980s to run the Advanced Research Projects Agency network (ARPANET). ARPANET was originally designed to allow the contractors to share expensive computer resources that many of them needed for a limited time on their projects (such as databases and the then very expensive graphics programs), but it quickly became a communication network as the people working on such projects found it a convenient way to communicate and collaborate electronically.

As time went on, ARPANET became too popular for the capacity of the hardware upon which it was based and too big for the addressing system provided for in the protocols. Addresses require a specified amount of computer memory; the network grew faster than the original addressing scheme had ever anticipated. It is similar to using the letters of the alphabet as addresses—if one-letter addresses are used, there can be twenty-six users before one runs out of unique identifiers. If two letters are used, then 676 unique addresses are possible, and so on. The addressing system has been expanded several times in the intervening years, and has grown into a layered system of (usually 3 letter) codes designating the network, sub-network, and particular local machine.

By itself, ARPANET was a large network. However, as more and more vendors and others working on government projects joined it, ARPANET became more than just a large network (a group of computers connected to each other) and took on more and more of the characteristics of an internetwork (a group of interconnected networks). An internet is any network of two or more computer networks. The Internet is "an internetwork of many networks all running the TCP/IP protocol suite, connected through gateways, and sharing common name and address spaces." In other words, the Internet is a particular internet, based largely in the United States but with connections world-wide, which allows computers at government agencies, educational institutions and corporations to communicate with each other and which facilitates resource-sharing and communication among the people who are able to log on to any of its constituent computers (called "hosts" or "nodes").

Another network, used heavily by educational institutions, is BITNET. There are gateways (computers that provide linkages) between BITNET and the Internet, but BITNET is not, properly speaking, part of the Internet. BITNET has its own addressing scheme and channels its messages through dedicated phone lines physically connecting adjacent computers. It, like the Internet, provides for resource sharing and communication and collaboration among its member schools, but it is primarily limited to educational institutions.

Today, the Internet and BITNET provide easy, fast, and generally reliable communication to researchers and scholars all over the world. Through the Internet, the library catalogs of an ever-growing number of college and university libraries are accessible. If an institution is going to have an online catalog and is going to allow people to dial in and access it by modem, it is a relatively simple thing to allow access over the Internet; many institutions have done this. Through BITNET and the Internet, discussion groups can be hosted on mainframes which allow, for example, catalogers in Richmond, VA to communicate with catalogers in Hong Kong, easily, economically, and almost instantaneously (certainly much faster than normal mail). Since the connections between the computers in the various networks and to the Internet are subsidized by the owners of the mainframe computers that are networked together, the cost to the individual person using the Internet is usually at most the price of a local telephone call.

To make the leap from the Internet as it exists today to the situation that David Brin conjures up in *Earth* could easily be accomplished in forty years. Some of the problems that exist on the Internet now in minor form have grown to problems of major proportions in *Earth* but at a rate that is believable in forty years. For example:

Privacy

Anyone who uses the Internet or BITNET now knows, if they think about it, that privacy is not a highly valued commodity in computer communications today. Every once in a while there will be a furor about censorship of this or that discussion list or bulletin board, but fundamentally computer mail is not a private medium, any more than CB radio is private. I subscribe to two discussion lists, and on an average of once every three weeks a note that is intended to be private (e.g. "What are you doing for lunch in San Francisco?") is mistakenly posted to the discussion list. Discussion list moderators and bulletin board system operators routinely edit postings for obscenity, illegality, or just plain boring content.

In Brin's vision, privacy even as a polite fiction is completely dead. One of the characters essentially commits suicide because what he had considered to be a private conversation was recorded and included in memoirs published on the world data net, and he has no other legal or moral recourse. Crime is virtually non-existent, because anyone with $8.50 to spend can buy a pair of "true-vue sensu-record goggles, with net access."[2] In an overpopulated society, almost any human interaction has been recorded by some bystander, who is only too happy to fax it to the police.

Although the world data net e-mail and private storage areas are supposed to be private, anyone with the necessary programming skills can steal access to another's private data. In fact, there is a cottage industry engaged in doing just that and another one engaged in defending data. However, there are apparently no laws to punish offenders in this area, and the societal taboo against secrecy regards expressed desires for privacy with suspicion.

Given the premise of the Helvetian War and the hatred of secrecy it engendered, this lack of concern for privacy is believable in the story. Given that wide use of computer networks is in its infancy and that the problem will only become worse as more people gain access to the Internet, now is the time to be working on solutions to the problem, or at least etiquette to handle *faux pas* gracefully.

---

2   Brin, p. 308.

Information Overload

Information overload has been the monster under the bed of librarianship since at least the fifties. It boggles the mind to contemplate the number of trees that have died for self-satisfied articles about librarians as "information professionals" who are increasingly needed in a paperless society. *Earth* presents a picture of information overload run amok, with the sufferers getting along quite nicely without an "information professional" in sight.

In *Earth,* publication is a relatively simple process. One creates a work, usually multi-media, and makes it available on the net. There is a system for automatically notifying anyone living who is mentioned in the work, but there seems to be no requirement that their permission be given before recorded images of them are included in the work.

Computer memory space is also not a problem. It is cheap and full-text (or image) storage is no problem. There are charges for access to some sources of information (such as real-time satellite images of disaster areas), but there seem to be no restrictions on who can access what and no practical limit on either an individual's or on the system's storage capacity.

Indeed, the problem isn't gaining access to information. The problem is screening out the irrelevant bits of information. There are artificial intelligence "personalities" who act as secretaries to screen the electronic mail (and answer the routine stuff) and there are programs called "ferrets," "foxes," and "bloodhounds" that people can send out into the net to retrieve information on whatever it is they want to know about. [Ed.: Have you used your personal information manager or checked with your gopher today?] Although these programs are available "off the shelf," the more effective ones are custom designed. Relevant information is one of the "perks" of the computer literate—a level of computer literacy that is largely limited to professional programmers in our world.

With all of this information, there appears to be little or no concern about the "pre-net" publications. One of the characters runs into an essay that is only available in "antique" hard copy form but, with such a mass of readily available information, it appears that no one worries about the unconverted works that are gradually being lost. Similarly, it seems to bother no one that new editions of a work can appear almost daily, and there is no evidence in the novel that anyone is particularly concerned about preserving the old editions.

We are facing some of this problem today, with the proliferation of electronic journals. We are grappling with the problem of how to provide access to them, who should preserve them in their various editions, and whether and for how long archives of discussion lists should be kept. Computer professionals are primarily concerned with backing up data so that it can be restored on another computer if the system goes down. They are not, by and large, concerned with preserving the data for scholars to track all the different forms that it appeared in. In *Earth*, when the system is temporarily disrupted, people react as we would if the phone service was temporarily interrupted. They do not appear to be concerned that the sum total of human knowledge (from their perspective) was in danger.

Copyright

Earth is not a legal treatise, nor does the plot involve court cases, but there is an interesting lack of concern for copyright in the characters' attitudes and actions. One character enhances, condenses, and expands entertainment videos, adding a dimension to make them holograms, adding special effects, tailoring them to the intended viewer's attention span. Her work is expensive because she does it well, but there is no mention of royalties or licensing payments being made as she changes and sells such things as "a lucrative 3-D reprocessing of the entire nine-hundred episode *Star Trek* saga, and all three *Rambo* movies."[3] The book raises interesting questions about how society will deal with compensation for people whose full texts appear on the Internet, possibly used by millions of people or possibly ignored by millions. Brin implies that there is some sort of accounting going on by the system automatically, and certainly royalties on such a system could be calculated automatically according to the number of people accessing the work.

The book raises the issue of ease of plagiarism and copyright violation as well. As anyone with a word processor or a graphics editor knows, text can be changed, added to, deleted; graphic images stored in a computer can be changed ("enhanced") to do things like altering photographs undetectably. At the present time, the Gutenberg Project (a project to provide machine-readable text for literary "classics") has chosen to deal with this issue by only converting works that are out of copyright. There is nothing now (except ethics enforced by public opinion) to keep someone from "enhancing" *Alice in Wonderland* and presenting it as their own work. [Ed.: My electronic version of *Alice* is copyrighted by the person who wrote the introduction and added some notes.] What will happen when the work of

---

3   Brin, p. 468.

living people starts being liable to "enhancement"? Particularly undetectable "enhancements"?

A related question, more directly tied to the growth of the Internet, is: what will happen as the desire of data vendors to restrict usage of the data (so that they can sell it to more customers) collides with the desire of libraries to provide access to information over the Internet?

There is nothing about the net in *Earth* that is inherently improbable. Brin provides us with a view of a possible future of the Internet and the networks which will succeed it. It is a wonderful piece of speculative fiction that raises interesting questions for librarians, "computer people," and society at large.

Kathy Fladland, Virginia Commonwealth University.
BITNET: kfladland@vcuvax.bitnet

The Transreal Experience

William M. Lidwell

Omniplan Corporation and University of Houston—Clear Lake

Kim J. Trull

University of Houston—Clear Lake

Imagine a cat that is neither alive nor dead. A cat that exists in an absolute, irreducible state of indeterminancy and probability. Not alive. Not dead. But a superposition of "aliveness" and "deadness"—a state of wonderful indecision and uncertainty representable only as probability. One more thing: the cat stays in this superposition of states until someone looks at it, at which time reality is forced to decide whether the cat is alive or dead. What would such a cat be like? What kind of reality could support such a beast? If you find the notion difficult, even absurd, don't feel bad. The notion is absurd—by design.

The late physicist Erwin Schrodinger described the cat in a now famous thought experiment designed to demonstrate the absurdity of quantum reality. The thought experiment, referred to as "Schrodinger's cat," is now believed to represent something much more profound: we are experientially unprepared to deal with the dynamics of quantum reality. The discordance between quantum reality and "macroreality" is so stark and disconcerting that many physicists have refused to accept it in the face of overwhelming evidence. Schrodinger himself stated, "I don't like it, and I'm sorry I ever had anything to do with it." Albert Einstein generated the famous quote, "God does not play dice with the universe." Niels Bohr captured these feelings with, "Anyone who is not shocked by quantum theory has not understood it."

Schrodinger's cat is a wonderful example of a transreal experience. Transreal experiences—experiences across realities—serve to conflict with, punctuate, or distort our understanding of our perceptions. The quantum cat is quite obviously an example of transreal conflict, a scarce phenomenon since experience with alternative realities has, to date, been limited. But what of a world where access to radically different realities is commonplace? How will transreal technology be used to augment "real" reality and what are the societal, psychological, and philosophical implications? How will transreal experiences alter our understanding of existence, knowledge, perception, and of course, reality?

The air in the park smelled sweet—Santiago found it hard to believe that it was merely an olfactory sensation created by the computer and fed through the helmet of his transreality bodysuit. As he pondered this marvel, he glanced down at his hand...

"Esteban! I'm a *cat*!" Santiago exclaimed to his unseen trainer.

"Yes," replied a disembodied voice. "The last user was running simulations on quantum physics. Your simulation isn't loaded yet, so I left that one running."

"Great! I've never been a cat before."

Suddenly, Santiago panicked. His vision doubled as his virtual paws began to vanish and reappear alternately—as if the program wasn't sure if he was there or not.

"I'm not just any cat—I'm a *quantum* cat!"

Click! Click! A low sound came from behind, as if someone had tossed pebbles on a sidewalk. Santiago turned. A stately, whitehaired man sat facing away from him, vigorously shaking something in his hands and then tossing it onto a nearby stone table. Dice!

Santiago's paws reappeared and he crept forward. The dice fell again, and his body disappeared. *Click! Click!* And it reappeared, although it did not seem as solid as before.

The man turned and gazed upon Santiago. Santiago's vision cleared and his paws returned to a comfortable opaqueness.

"Ah, yes! The cat," replied the old man. "Nice to SEE you again," he said with a giggle.

"Wha...?"

"This is the quantum world, my friend. Everything here exists only as probabilities," his grin widened. "You are but a roll of the dice until I look upon you. You owe neither life nor death to me, for here each are but mere probabilities. Your precious existence requires some gratitude, though, for without a kindly glance cast in your direction, your atoms would just as soon remain undecided. An observation to take the dice out of your diet, if you will."

"How can I exist, yet not exist? Dice out of my diet? I'm not sure that I understand..."

"Santiago," the tone of the man's voice changed as he spoke. "Your simulation is loaded and will begin immediately. This one is now over."

"But Esteban..." Santiago sighed as one reality suddenly faded into the weightlessness of lowearth orbit.

The "zerog" experience is as remarkable as it is alien. As organisms evolved to exist in a gravitybased environment, nothing in our Earthbound experience has prepared us for the airless freefall of space. This is not to suggest that efforts to simulate zerog on Earth are nonexistent—astronaut training, for example, averages thousands of dollars per hour utilizing a large water tank or WETF (weightless environment training facility) and KC135s simulating weightlessness during parabolic flights. These simulations, however, have serious limitations: the WETF simulates the weightlessness, but not the physics (water, unlike space, is a rather thick medium); and the KC135s provide a maximum of 30 seconds of zerog at a time. Hence, longterm zerog simulation—the kind astronauts will ideally need in order to prepare for space station assembly—is unavailable here on Earth.

Can longduration, authentic zerog simulation exist on Earth? The variables involved in creating such simulations are threefold: (1) time, (2) weightlessness, and (3) physics. Drop towers (freefalling elevators) and parabolic flights provide the weightlessness and physics, but are grossly lacking in duration. The WETF provides an effective longduration weightless environment, but fails to effectively simulate the physics. Transreal technology could potentially provide effective longduration simulations which accurately depict the physics of a true, zerog environment. It would, however, fail to overcome the conflicting stimuli which remind the user that he or she is not 150 miles above the Earth, but rather on the Earth, both feet planted, wearing a rather unwieldy VR system.

This type of transreal experience occurs when sensory faculties perceive stimuli which are out of alignment; for example, I perceive that I am floating above the Earth visually, aurally, etc., but the tactile sensors in my feet record a pressure consistent with standing upright. Transreal experiences like this certainly challenge our abilities to adapt and innovate our mental models of the way reality works, but in the case of creating simulations, such conflicts need to be suppressed. Reality is, afterall, no more than consistency. Consistency of the senses. Consistency of our memories. And, consistency between our memories and our senses. It is when inconsistencies arise that reality becomes less real—or, more properly, less familiar. Thus, an effective, longterm zerog experience will require either the elimination of gravity, or, more likely, the elimination of the sensation of gravity.

A pen floated free of a pocket. Santiago reached for it, lost control, and flew against the wall of lockers. Unfamiliar to the absence of gravity, he had exerted too much force in his reach.

"Almost time to dock with the station," Esteban reminded him.

"On my way." Santiago pushed from a locker and flew through the narrow craft, marvelling at the simulated experience. Reaching a control panel, he struggled to get his feet into supporting straps, and looked out a nearby window.

A cloudstreaked Earth seemed to fill Santiago's vision. A dark blot appeared on the distant curve of the globe as the space station came into view. Meanwhile, 3dimensional holograms of both his spacecraft and the station appeared, orbiting above the control panel.

Santiago removed a pair of gloves from a drawer and pulled them over his hands and connected their trailing wires to sockets on the control panel. He flexed his fingers and the sensors lining the gloves sent test patterns to the control panel, which beeped at Santiago, signalling that the gloves were working properly.

Reaching his hands into the holographic display, Santiago grabbed the miniature spacecraft with a gentle hand. He felt it—like a solid model held between his fingers. Gently, he turned the craft, aligning its airlock with a docking port on one side of the space station. Santiago felt the motion of the spacecraft under his feet, and out of the corner of his eye he saw the Earth move out of sight. Satisfied that the alignment was correct, he brought the holographic craft closer to the miniature station. Carefully, he brought them together until he felt a *click!* The two had met.

With a sigh, Santiago released the model spacecraft and withdrew his hands. He'd done it. He had successfully docked his craft to an orbiting station.

"Very good!" Esteban almost sang. "One of your best docking maneuvers."

"What was the deviation from target dock lockon? Was it less than 5 degrees?" Santiago asked.

A moment of silence. "Roger, that," said Esteban, "3.5 degrees. Outstanding!"

"Whew! I have never docked in zerog before. It was nothing like the simulations at the academy."

"They didn't have SDTs (sensory deprivation tanks) at the academy, Santiago."

Santiago leaned back and caught sight of the Earth below. He turned and focused on the spiraling whiteness named "Marie," just a few hundred miles from his hometown. Was his family safe? Did they go to a shelter? His thoughts raced.

Thoughts are interesting phenomena. They are personal in the sense that we generate them, but they often remind us that they retain an air of independence—a dream in which we have no control or, perhaps the solution to a difficult problem magically suggesting itself long after we have ceased thinking about it. Thoughts instill us with the confidence that we know and understand reality on one level, and yet remind us that they are, themselves, no more than the thoughtassisted translations of stimuli past. Ultimately, our knowledge and perception of reality exist as intimate threads within that same metaphysical fabric.

This realization suggests that transreal technology represents more than a new development in simulation or entertainment; it suggests an extension of our already active role in the construction of reality. Presently, the "objective" stimuli perceived by our senses impose a syntax on our translations of what reality means. Transreal technology, however, permits the construction of environments in which the stimuli are, in principle, completely controllable by the perceiver—as in the preCopernican universe, reality, once again, revolves around the person. The epistemological and ontological questions of old reemerge: what is reality? what can we know of it? what is our place in it? Questions argued in the abstract for thousands of years become the object of controlled, empirical enquiry. Transreal technology, as result, will represent the first, true empirical medium for studying the fundamental epistemological and ontological questions of reality and our roles within it.

What answers lie within the transreal experience? Perhaps we will discover the neutral, deterministic universe of Newton: clean, objective, and mechanical. Or, perhaps, we will again discover our quantum cat lounging about in his probabilistic world, watching the dice, and anxiously waiting to be perceived. Regardless, reality will no longer be selfevidently real, perception no longer selfevidently accurate. Transreal experiences will likely not provide all the answers, but they will provide the most experientially challenging and intellectually enlightening phenomena ever encountered by human beings—they might very well lead the greatest ontological and epistemological revolutions since Copernicus and Darwin.

Santiago watched as the moon disappeared behind the horizon, travelling its perfectly circular orbit around the Earth.

He stood on the edge of a virtual cliff. The Earth revolving below and nothing but a sheer, empty drop between it and the spacecraft in which he stood. In a moment of panic mixed with excitement, he hesitated. Taking a deep breath, he closed his eyes and stepped out...

But there was no fall. At least not the fiery plummet towards Earth that his brain had envisioned in its panic. Instead, he felt the gentle pull of Earth's gravity on his body, pulling him as he floated from the spacecraft, taking him into an orbit like a tiny, human moon.

With a deep sigh, Santiago relaxed and felt along the arm of his maneuvering unit. He pressed a button on one side and turned away from the Earth. Now he saw a seemingly endless space, broken only by the bright glare of sunlight bouncing off of the malfunctioning remote sensing satellite. He moved closer.

Suddenly, the satellite vanished! A loud roar boomed somewhere nearby and Santiago spun around. No Earth! Nothing! Only blackness. Total darkness.

"Esteban!" he screamed. "What's happening?"

Esteban didn't answer.

Alice Grumann sat up and removed the helmet of her transreality suit. She shook her head to free it from the heavy, hazy cobwebs that seemed to fill it. The room remained dark around her with only a faint glow entering through the window. She eased her legs over the edge of the sensory deprivation tank and stood.

"Oh, Esteban!" she murmured, laying a hand on the computer sitting nearby. "I hope the power outage didn't hurt you."

Distant thunder and the soft tapping of rainfall on the window. Alice sighed and pulled a blanket from her bed. Wrapping it about her, she walked over and stared out the window. She put a hand on the glass, half thinking to reach through and calm the trees swaying in the garden. The cool pane of the window stopped her hand. Indifferent, raindrops continued their steady drum against the glass.

William M. Lidwell is an Instructional Systems Designer with Omniplan Corporation and Senior Research Associate with the Advanced Knowledge Transfer Group at the University of Houston—Clear Lake. He is well published and is actively researching in the cognitive sciences.

Kim J. Trull is an Academic Computing Laboratory Supervisor at the University of Houston—Clear Lake. She is completing her M.S. in Studies of the Future at the University of Houston—Clear Lake. Internet: trull@cl4.cl.uh.edu

Transcendence at the Interface:
The Architecture of Cyborg Utopia
—or—
Cyberspace Utopoids as
Postmodern Cargo Cult

David Porush

Rensselaer Polytechnic Institute

The emotional power of video games draws heavily on the computer's power within that supports a simulated world and a meditative environment, what [one user] calls a place for "recentering." But the power of the games draws on other aspects of the computer as well, some of them resonant with children's fascination with computer toys as "metaphysical machines." As a computational object, the video game holds out two promises. The first is a touch of infinity—the promise of a game that never stops.... [The second is] ... the promise of perfection.[1]

Liminality is the realm of the primitive hypothesis, where there is a certain freedom to juggle with the factors of existence.[2]

---

1   Sherry Turkle, *The Second Self: Computers and the Human Spirit* (New York: Simon and Schuster, 1984) 88,89.

2   Victor Turner, "Betwixt and Between: The Liminal Period in *Rites De Passage*," *Proceedings of the American Ethnological Society Symposium on New Approaches to the Study of Religion* (1964) 4-20.

Introduction: Utopia and the Cyborg

The way to get to utopia is to model your view of human nature and then invent a technology to control or direct that model—whether a political technology like the one Thomas Hobbes portrays in his *Leviathan*, a biological technology as in Aldous Huxley's *Brave New World*, a psychological technology as in B. F. Skinner's *Walden Two*, epistemo-technologies, as in Bacon's *The New Atlantis*, information technologies as in Orwell's *1984*, or just plain old technology generally, as in H.G. Wells' *A Modern Utopia*. I call these utopian visions "technologies" because they are deterministic in all senses of that word: systems that seek and believe in perfect control. When the human is inserted into the utopian system, the result is a feedback loop, in which the system encourages the "best" part and controls the "worst" part of human nature, while the human, in return, maintains the system with material, energy, information, flesh, and spirit.

In other words, the result of the inscription of a utopian vision onto a human is a *cyborg*: a natural organism linked for its survival and improvement to a cybernetic system. Of all the great utopianists, Sir Thomas More, Francis Bacon, Campanella, Restif de la Bretonne, Locke, Rousseau..., it is Thomas Hobbes in *Leviathan* (1651) who understands the essentially cyborg quality of utopia.

> [S]eeing [that] life is but a motion of limbs, the beginning whereof is in some principal part within, why may we not say that all automata (engines that move themselves by springs and wheels as doth a watch) have an artificial life? For what is the heart but a spring, and the nerves but so many strings; and the joints but so many wheels giving motion to the whole body such as was intended by the Artificer? Art goes yet further, imitating that rational and most excellent work of nature, man. For by art is created that great Leviathan called a Common wealth or a State [in Latin, *civitas*] which is but an artificial man, though of greater stature and strength.[3]

Scratch the model for a utopia and you get a blueprint of human nature. As we revise our technologic, different versions of utopia become imaginable, which in turn are fed by and feed into different versions of the human, which in turn are fed by and feed into new technologies, and so on, creating a feedback loop the byproduct of which is an ever more sophisticated version

---

3   Thomas Hobbes, *Leviathan* (1651).

of the cyborg, whose generations can be measured by the turns of this spiralling loop.

The blueprint of human nature has always been subject to revision. But never as radically as now, when our own utopian technologies are physically transcribing themselves onto our bodies and re-creating the human in their own image, or forcing our evolution into what many have come to call the "posthuman" through a combination of mechanistic and genetic-biological manipulations. In short, the posthuman is the inscription of the ultimate controlling technology onto the human, the cybernetic technologies of selfhood, of mental identity, of cognition, of the mind, of intelligence itself, of communication, of language, and of The Code. To that extent, we are all cyborgs already, controlled by the systems we've embraced or which have embraced and defined us through our media, our computers, our systems of communication. For this reason, virtual reality, or *cyberspace*, is the perfect expression of postmodern trends.

Cyberspace as Nostalgia for Sacramental Space

Cyberspace visions form a self-reflexive complex of discourses about redefining and re-inscribing the human within a pure space.[4] They evolve from the postmodern technologies which aim at modelling human nature—and manipulating it—through computational mechanisms, thereby representing the culmination of cybernetic technologies that threaten most humanist positions. To get there requires jacking in to some machine-body system, an implicitly cyborg movement. So cyberspace becomes really interesting, not when you see it as an extension of video games or television or the suburban shopping mall, but as a robust, recurrent, and fundamental ideal of humanity hardwired into our genetic code—and perhaps even our physiological code—finally finding a technology through which it can express itself fully: the desire to leave the body but keep the mind. As a consequence, many commentators think that cyberspace represents utopian possibilities.

Yet in my view, those who suggest that cyberspace is utopia enact a primordial, and probably compulsory, form of cultural mysticism no different from cargo cults that erect towers of trash to summon the airplane gods, an expression of the enduring human compulsion to create a transcendental architecture, as if the right restructuring or reconfiguration of space, time, matter, and information will bring heaven down to earth. The projection of

---

4   John Christie, "Cyberspace as Cartesian" in *Literature Towards the Year 2000 and After: Cyberpunk* edited by George Slusser (University of Georgia Press, forthcoming).

utopian wishes onto cyberspace represents a nostalgic desire to return to some sacramental space. After all, cyberspace, like other heavens, won't really be a place, but rather the simulation of a place, a virtual space.

Cyberspace is a metaphysical technology.

Claims for Cyberspace Utopia

William Gibson's trilogy *Neuromancer* (1984), *Count Zero* (1986), and *Mona Lisa Overdrive* (1988), gave us both the word cyberspace and its most compelling descriptions. Despite his initially dystopian vision, Gibson also portrays cyberspace as a site for the release of imaginings, unconscious desires, heroic adventure, and even transcendence forbidden and sterilized in the real "meat" world where bodies have to eat.[5] Gibson's heroes flee from the pedestrian and cannibal world to find salvation and even transcendence in cyberspace, among cognitively, and eventually spiritually, provocative virtual beings who exist only in this nether world of the data matrix and software constructs. Many of the reasons for the utopian view of cyberspace have to do with the way it reorients the mind to the experience of information *bodilessly*. One of Gibson's most striking descriptions of cyberspace is the "bodiless exultation" of those who inhabit it.

The Cyberspace Movement—and it is beginning to take on the proportions of a capital M Movement—has something millennial about it, focussing irrationally on an innovation that is still quite illusory, not to say technically improbable. Here at the end of the second millennium, we seem to have exhausted and poisoned this irremediable material world. Perhaps we yearn for an unspoiled place. Two large Cyberspace Conferences[6] sponsored papers by researchers in AI, the cognitive sciences, hardware and software development, architecture, sociology, psychology, the arts, education, media centers, defense department, NASA, philosophy, history and literary studies, as well as about a dozen corporations. A list of their discussions of cyberspace reveals a common thread of utopianism: C will renovate human relations; it will unite art and technology; it will represent an altogether new and radical domain for improved social, psychic, and

---

5   For a larger exploration of this tension see David Porush, "Cybernauts in Cyberspace: William Gibson's *Neuromancer*" in *Aliens: The Anthropology of Science Fiction*, edited by George E. Slusser and Eric Rabkin. (Carbondale, Illinois: Southern Illinois University Press, 1987).

6   The first in Austin, Texas, in May 1990, and the second in Santa Cruz, California, in May 1991.

perceptual transactions. Bypassing the infirmities of the body, cyberspace will free the cripple and liberate the paralytic. Enabling multimedia and sensory access to the entire wealth of world data, cyberspace will deliver a universal education. Through its anonymity, cyberspace will invite the construction of a more ethical code and create norms for human interaction that strip distinctions of gender, class, race and power. C will provide a playspace for the imagination to roam free, having liberated the mind from its inevitably neurotic relationship to the body. C therefore has untold psychotherapeutic possibilities.[7] Yet C will incapacitate destructive urges and consequences by removing our bodies. Cyberspace will create the means for a pure and perfect democracy and universal suffrage in which everyone can vote immediately on any issue. C will present the possibilities for "Virtual communities."[8] C will reconstruct the nature of the relationship between labor and time and labor and space and reconstruct authoritarian techniques as they are manifested in the workplace[9]—although one wonders who's going to empty the garbage and build the roads after we've all emigrated to this new virtual suburb. While C will undoubtedly present new opportunities for criminality, rape or physical assault will become impossible. C will present a new opportunity for our manifest destiny, a new frontier.[10] C will make war obsolete by turning it into A Desert Storm Videogame.[11] Cyberspace will create a totalized hypertextual platform which will cure what ails American higher education.[12] C will enable us to combine work and play in a new way and to make wars obsolete. Even the music will be better there. Cyberspace will be the new, clean, virtual Eden where we'll all emigrate to when this physical world becomes an unlivable ecodisaster. In cyberspace we will finally perfect the academic's dream of sex: we'll be able

7   Kenneth Lee Diamond, "The Psychotherapeutic Possibilities of Cyberspace." Unpublished paper delivered at 1st Annual Conference on Cyberspace, Austin, Texas, May 1990.

8   Joseph Arthur Hunt, Ellen Putner Hunt, and Tony DeLeon at 1st Annual Conference on Cyberspace, Austin, Texas, May 1990.

9   Pam Rosenthal, "Cyberspace: Utopian Workspaces in a Dystopian World." Unpublished paper, delivered at 2nd Annual Conference on Cyberspace, Santa Cruz, California, May 1991.

10   Chip Morningstar at 2nd Annual Conference on Cyberspace, Santa Cruz, California, May 1991.

11   James Der Derian, "Cyberwar, Videogames, and the New World Order."

12   I confess I'm responsible for this one: "Toward the Hyperversity: The Hyperlibrary at the Heart of the Postmodern University," 1990 Rensselaer internal memorandum.

to do it without the messiness of our bodies.[13] (Perhaps I should have said the dream of sex that's academic!)

All these claims are equally enticing and ludicrous, plausible and impossible, hopeful and naive. The slick surfaces of Gibson's gleaming prose excites in almost every reader a romantic desire for a new and cleaner stage for heroic action. Reading *Neuromancer* induces a hankering for the possibilities of a new frontier to replace our dream of space exploration which has been shattered by bureaucratic thumbsucking. And after all, the allure of a whole new world, a world evolved out of this one, invented to our specs, completely artificial, completely deterministic in its platform for unpredictable in its degrees of freedom, is irresistible. But most of those who succumb to this latent romantic ideal in the cyberspace fiction forget that Gibson's work is distinctly *dystopian*, filled with dread and a disorienting loss of memory and hope. It's as if engineers in 1948, excited by Orwell's *1984*, started developing technologies of continuous and total surveillance. Cyberspace as Gibson conceived it is a sort of hell (or at best a sort of limbo or purgatory) where not-beings are subjected to excruciating experiments on the boundary between hallucination and bodiless exultation: a nightmarish configuration of technology, death, and the unconscious against which the *Neuromancer* trilogy warns us even as it invites us to play there.

Transcendence at the Interface

Nonetheless, there is one moment in *Neuromancer* that is most striking for it is beyond utopian; it is transcendent. Case, the hero, jacks into cyberspace to confront the new creature Wintermute/Neuromancer, whom he has helped evolve. Wintermute decides to present himself as a face, which Case now confronts at the interface. The face speaks:

"I'm not Wintermute now."

"So what are you." He drank from the flask, feeling nothing.

"I'm the matrix, Case."

Case laughed. "Where's that get you?"

"Nowhere. Everywhere. I'm the sum total of the works, the whole show."

"That's what [your inventor] wanted?"

"No. She couldn't imagine what I'd be like." The yellow smile [on the screen] widened.

---

13 Jean Claude Guedon takes a little more serious view of this in his presentation at the 2nd Annual Conference on Cyberspace, Santa Cruz, California, May 1991.

"So what's the score? How are things different? You running the world now? You God?"

"Things aren't different. Things are things."[14]

The brash human approaches the godmind he has helped release, here deep in gloaming of cyberspace, and the reader must consider deeper questions summoned by this spell: is transcendence in cyberspace be an illusion? Or can the machine be a means to communicating with gods? Will cyberspace finally provide us with a true *deus ex machina*? Can there be transcendence at the interface?

The Invention of the Transcendental Architecture

The intersection between the transcendent world and this one creates or requires an architecture which ultimately restructures society itself. Humans inevitably feel that a certain architecture is needed to summon the transcendent into this world.

The reverse is also true: when the correct architecture is constructed, the transcendent will be compelled to inhabit it willy nilly. "Build it and they will come."

This is an irresistible complex for any culture. Hopi, Babylonians, Aztecs, Ainu, ... all construct their worldmaps and temples and landing strips for the gods. Judaeo-Christian culture marks the moment when it invents the *architecture of the transcendent* with a striking self-contradiction in the text of the *Bible*. This contradiction signals the moment that Western civilization turns from natural transcendentalism to an *architectonic* transcendentalism, of which cyberspace is the most far-flung expression. *Exodus* 25 says, "*Do not make of Me gods of silver, or gods of gold. An altar of earth shalt thou make unto Me ... In every place where I cause My name to be mentioned I will come unto you and bless thee. And if thou make Me an altar of stone, thou shalt not build it of hewn stones; for if thou lift up thy tool upon it, thou hast profaned it. Neither shalt thou go up by steps unto Mine altar, that thy nakedness be uncovered.*" The intention seems simple enough here: "I can be worshipped anywhere. A lazy pile of rocks on the raw earth will do, thank you very much."

Only five brief chapters later, however, in *Exodus* 25-27, we read elaborate and mathematical specifications for the Ark of the Covenant and the Temple to contain it, with excruciatingly exact demands for the ark,

---

14   William Gibson, *Neuromancer* (New York: Ace Books, 1984) 269-270.

the table, the tabernacle, the curtains on the tabernacle, the tent around the curtains, and a veil to cover the tent, then a door into the veil and a screen for the veil, a courtyard around the whole thing.

What could be less in the spirit of the simple design for an altar of casual stones a few chapters ago than this fetishistic elaboration of a blueprint for the Holy Sepulchre? Ten or twelve centuries of civilization which intervened between the composition of *Exodus* 20 and the accretion of *Exodus* 25 when the *Bible* is recompiled after the Babylonian exile. In those thousand years, the Jews invented the idea that we can summon what was lost by creating the correct architecture, if only we surround the intangible with this elaborate stagecraft, the proper *deus ex machina*.

From Transcendental Architecture to Transcendental ArchiTEXTure

When the Temple was destroyed and the Jews dispersed, this compulsion to create an architecture around the holy text was transformed, enfolded into the text itself. Because there was no Temple, ritual sacrifice was abandoned, a ceremony inherited from nomadic days and elaborated upon in the architectural period. The hegemony of the Priests was broken, a social and political development in its way as revolutionary as our modern democratic revolutions since they ruled by birthright and caste. Rabbis took their place: the poor grad student types devoted to rewriting (literally) and re-inscribing (interpreting) the text of the laws. They introduced the most profound cultural innovation: an architecture surrounding the *Torah*, something much more portable, yet profoundly more potent, an epistemology of interpretation, a cognitive manner of reading and scholarship that ultimately produces systems within systems of commentary that turn literal into metaphorical and metaphorical into meta-metaphorical and then back into literal again in a twenty-century accretion of polysemous and cross-referencing commentary, footnotes, exegesis, numerology, marginalia, embroidery, folklore, interpretation, and feedback-looping dialectic. The result is archi*texture*: the *Talmud*. The reader hooked to this system finds it does very different things to his head. It was already going cybernetic back then.

The Great Leap

Cyberspace is a further step on the same evolutionary road, both an analog of the transformation from Temple to *Talmud*, and one enabled by that ancient autopoetic leap across the bifurcation from architecture to archi*texture*.

The innovation of the Jews for Western culture was to send out a new sort of invitation to transcendence: "Come, spirit, enter this world not through a doorway of matter, but through an architexture of thought and information. *The most portable altar of all is in your head, man, and in your words. Build it, write the right story, utter the right glamour/grammar, and They will come.*" It was already cybernetic.

It has taken us ten more centuries to get there, but technology and the accidents of intellectual history have brought us to the point when we are ready to take the next step. What lies on the line that begins in an earthen altar, proceeds through transcendental architecture, and leaps from a transcendental arrangement of signs? Cyberspace represents a thrust at the illuminated landscape beyond textuality, where information suffers no mediation whatsoever and the soaring cognitive dome of the brain itself becomes the interface and the sensory text of cyberspace. And all of us who have answered the siren call of artificial intelligence just can't shake that feeling: something's waiting for us on the other side.

If cyberspace is utopian it is because it opens the possibility of using the deterministic platform for unpredictable ends (as the laws of chaos are teaching us is possible), launching us into ever-higher orders of complexity as we fluctuate non-linearly in this far-from-equilibrium cyborg system. Perhaps, who knows, we might even grow a system large and complex and unstable enough to leap across that last of all possible bifurcations—*autopoetically*—into that strangest of all possible attractors, the godmind, just as Gibson predicts. It's pretty to think so, anyway. And both comforting and dismaying that even as postmoderns we still labor under these irresistible delusions.

David Porush is professor of interdisciplinary literary studies and co-director for Autopoeisis, an AI research project in story generation at Rensselaer Polytechnic Institute in Troy, NY. He is the author of *The Soft Machine: Cybernetic Fiction*. Internet: porusd@rpi.edu

Virtual Reality in Medicine and Medical Education

Cheryl S. Pace

Archie R. Dykes Library
University of Kansas Medical Center

> In 1986 and 1987, I started getting telephone calls from people who had read about my research and wanted to know if they could apply virtual environments to problems in their own fields. ... People working with cerebral palsied patients wondered whether tongue-steered VR could free trapped minds from dysfunctional bodies. Anesthesiologists wanted a better way of displaying vital signs from all the instruments they had to monitor—the surgical theater is getting like a jet cockpit that way.—Thomas Furness (Rheingold, *Virtual Reality*, p.209)

Computers and related technology are widely used in the health care field to monitor patients, and to assist in diagnosis and treatment. The current development of virtual reality technologies will enhance many of these applications and will promote a variety of new medical innovations. It will also affect not only the health care patients but also a wide range of health care professionals: physicians, surgeons, nurses, psychologists, rehabilitation specialists, researchers, pharmacists, educators, and bioengineers. But, perhaps even more important, many of these potential uses of virtual reality will also directly affect *you* when you are a patient.

Imagine that you are going to be admitted to the hospital for several days to have some tests run. You've never been in the hospital before and, even though you are optimistic about the test results, the idea of staying in the hospital frightens you. Or imagine that your child has been diagnosed with a chronic illness and that you are now faced with regular visits to the hospital for treatment. Both you and your child are nervous and afraid and worry about what it will be like. In both of these situations, much of the fear is the concern about the unknown. A walk through the hospital or even through the operating room could alleviate some of this anxiety, but staffing constraints and access restrictions make casual walkthroughs unrealistic. Fortunately, virtual reality will offer the opportunity to visit such restricted environments and can provide the reassurance that such a personal exploration of the hospital can bring. Using virtual reality technology, you could even "spend a night" in the hospital, watch the operation you are going to have, or actually experience a particular treatment before it happens in "real time."

Medical imaging technology is already quite advanced, but images are still twodimensional. Xrays show only a single "slice." CAT scans provide consecutive slices that can be assembled into mosaic presentations. And, ultrasound, too, is only twodimensional. Using virtual reality (VR), however, these actual diagnostic images of a patient could be used to create a threedimensional model of the patient. The potential use of these "scientific imaging" models in medical diagnosis, treatment planning, and education will revolutionize the field. The benefits of determining the location of tumors, the placement of surgical incisions, or practicing difficult surgical procedures ahead of time are of inestimable value.

If a physician were wearing a headmounted VR display that showed these diagnostic images while looking at the patient, it would almost be like wearing "xray glasses." For example, if an ultrasound scanner was hooked up to a headmounted display, the physician could see the image superimposed on the patient's body rather than having to consult a nearby screen. Already planning for radiation treatment benefits from virtual reality support. The goal of radiation treatment is to deliver a lot of radiation to a tumor while minimizing the radiation exposure to healthy tissue. A "virtual body" of the patient can be created that allows the physician to visualize (before actual treatment) the location of the radiation beam in relation to the tumor and to the surrounding healthy tissue. This creates the opportunity to experiment with different approaches until the best one is identified. Obviously it would be counterproductive to do this directly with the patient!

Virtual reality is also a powerful tool for training people at various task, and the possibilities for its use in medical education are very exciting. Conceptually, virtual reality can be seen as an extension of multimedia. The threedimensional virtual bodies previously mentioned are ideal for learning anatomy, practicing physical examinations, testing diagnostic procedures, or even practicing ones's "bedside techniques." Virtual reality allows a student repeatedly to simulate skills that are difficult (if not dangerous) to practice in the real world. For example, surgical activities that involve fine motor skills when using the hands on live tissues and organs. In the future, not only will virtual reality mimic the complete medical procedure involving such matters as placement of organs within the patient, but even the way the scalpel will feel when cutting through different tissues.

Another interesting possibility is to use virtual reality to create an environment that can be shared by several people. This would enable a teacher to be present to provide immediate feedback during the learning process. Procedures that require the work of a team are ideally suited for practicing in a virtual reality environment.

The potential applications of virtual reality for the disabled are almost limitless. For example, interactive virtual reality systems could be used to restore motor power (within the virtual world) to individuals with physical handicaps who wish to "escape" a world that is defined by a bed or a wheelchair. Imagine the excitement of a child with a disability, dependent on a wheelchair, when he "plays" football with his friends for the first time.

The complexities of medical VR go beyond the mere technological issues. The associated ethical issues will also be compellingly significant. The accuracy of the representations created by the computer, the skill of the designer, and the preferences of the physician are all limiting factors in the validity of the reality that is possible.

Although the patient may have a choice among several virtual reality environments, that choice is likely to be more accommodating than in daily life. And what if the patient chooses to spend more time in the "virtual world" than in the "real world"? Could the virtual reality experience be addictive? Will alternative realities seduce people into being hypochondriacs?

Virtual reality is also a valuable tool in the development of therapeutic drugs. During this process, researchers look for targets or areas on proteins where molecules of a specific drug will attach themselves. Imagine trying to find the right molecular key to fit into a unique molecular lock. If a chemical can be found that makes such a fit on the protein found on a tumor cell or a pathogenic bacterium, then that chemical is potentially useful in drug development.

Virtual reality techniques allow the experimenter to create computer-generated models of the receptor sites within a human protein while another model represents the atoms of a potential drug. A researcher then manipulates the two models, moving the drug around the protein until it binds with it. The system not only displays a visual "docking" of the molecules, but it also provides feedback that allows the researcher to feel the magnitude of attraction and repulsion between the molecules. Such a molecular docking system exists at the University of North Carolina at Chapel Hill where much of the research on virtual reality in medicine is being done. Molecular docking systems also have potential in future protein design, including possible use in mapping the genetic code.

Virtual reality provides the opportunity to create controllable, repeatable environments. This technology can be used throughout the practice of medicine: to educate both patients and future health care practitioners, to practice surgical skills and diagnostic techniques, to enhance diagnosis and aid in treatment planning, and to design therapeutic drugs. As virtual reality technology is refined, its use in medicine is bound to increase dramatically.

References

"Being and Believing: Ethics of Virtual Reality," *Lancet*, 338(8762):2834 (3 August 1991).

H. McLellan, "Virtual Environments and Situated Learning," *Multimedia Review*, 3037 (Fall 1991).

Howard Rheingold, *Virtual Reality* (New York: Summit Books, 1991).

G. Stix, "Reach Out. Touch Is Added to Virtual Reality Simulations," *Scientific American*, 264(2):134 (February 1991).

D. L. Wheeler, "Computercreated World of Virtual Reality Opening New Vistas to Scientists," *The Chronicle of Higher Education*, 37(26):A6,12,13 (31 March 1991).

Cheryl Pace works at the Archie R. Dykes Library of the University of Kansas Medical Center. BITNET: csp07321@ukanvm.bitnet

Cyberpunk
Librarians . . .

Cyberpunks use all available data input to think for themselves.

You know who they are.

Every stage of history has produced a name and a heroic legend for the strong, stubborn, creative individual who explores some future frontier, collects and brings back new information, and offers to guide the gene pool to the next stage. Typically, the time maverick combines bravery with high curiosity, with super-self-esteem. These three talents are considered necessary for those engaged in the profession of genetic guide, a.k.a. philosopher.

...

Cyberpunks are the inventors, innovative writers, techno-frontier artists, risk-taking film directors, icon-shifting composers, expressionist artists, free-agent scientists, innovative show-biz entrepreneurs, techno-creatives, computer visionaries, elegant hackers, bit-blipping *Prolog* adepts, special effectives, video wizards, neurological test pilots, media explorers—all of those who boldly package and steer ideas out there where no thoughts have gone before.

Cyberpunks are sometimes authorized by the governors. They can with sweet cynicism and patient humor, interface their singularity with institutions. They often work within "the governing systems" on a temporary basis.

As often as not, they are unauthorized.
Timothy Leary, "The Individual as Reality Pilot" in *Storming the Reality Studio* edited by Larry McCaffery (Durham: Duke University Press, 1991), 245, 253.

Thinking Robots
An Aware Internet
and
Cyberpunk Librarians

Knowbot Explorations in Similarity Space

Martin Halbert

Fondren Library
Rice University

A library conversation in 2010

Participants:
 Carmen, a philosophy professor
 Tamara, a cognitive science graduate student
 David, a reference librarian.

Carmen: Tamara, I thought you were going to the library to work on the literature review for your thesis research, not to play video games.

Tamara: Oh! Hi, Dr. Rodriguez, you startled me. But, I AM working on....

Carmen: I'm just your thesis advisor, not your den mother. I'll see you later.

Tamara: No, wait! It really isn't a video game, I'm doing an online search of *Philosopher's Index*.

Carmen: Looks more like you're flying over Mars.

Tamara: No, that "planet" is *Philosopher's Index*. I'm not making this up! That's just how the database looks on this workstation....

David: How's everything going with the search, Tamara?

Tamara: David, I'm glad you came back! I'd like you to meet my thesis advisor, Dr. Carmen Rodriguez. I was just trying to explain to her that I'm doing an online literature search.

David: That's right, Dr. Rodriguez, she's searching a similarity space visualization of a philosophy database.

Carmen: Hmm. I don't remember online searches looking like video games when I did my doctoral research.

David: These holographic simulations are very new. Would you like a quick demonstration of how it works?

Carmen: Sure, you've piqued my curiosity. Could you tell me first of all what we're looking at? The holographic monitor Tamara is using seems to show the surface of some kind of electronically simulated alien world. And what are the other spherical things that look like psychedelic planets hanging in the black sky?

David: All of them are graphical representations of literature databases. The program Tamara is using can present data in a variety of formats, including this "planetscape" type. The program is called a similarity space visualizer.

Carmen: Hold on, back up and explain a few things. I haven't come to the library for an online literature search in several years, but what I remember getting were reams and reams of paper printouts of citations that matched keywords I gave the librarians. I had to sift through all the irrelevant citations looking for the good ones.

David: If you haven't had a search done for you in the last few years, I think you'll be pleasantly surprised. Online searching has advanced quite a bit lately. One of the main things the new systems are good at is prioritizing the output retrieved in terms of relevance to your query.

Carmen: How do they do that?

David: The new similarity comparison systems can statistically compare the words in the database documents to both your initial query and sample documents that you identify as relevant. Then they produce an output list ranked in descending order from most relevant to least relevant.

Carmen: That sounds pretty complicated. I'm not a computer programmer.

David: You don't have to be. The software handles all the complicated and tedious parts. At most, all you have to do is answer simple yes or no questions the system prompts you with. Here, let me show you a practical example, the search I helped Tamara with today. And let me also introduce you to the search tool we used, which is called a knowbot.

Carmen: A knowbot? What's that?

David: Knowbots are programs which collect information from network databases and organize it for you. Tamara and I created a knowbot this morning to do the literature review for her thesis.

Carmen: I gather that a knowbot isn't a physical robot. But what is it, exactly? How do you make one?

David: The same way you set up a spreadsheet or an electronic mail message, on the computer. A knowbot, like a spreadsheet, is basically a collection of data that you use the computer to manipulate and produce new information. A knowbot is a bit more sophisticated, in that it can also make decisions and recommendations for you, like an expert system. In fact a knowbot is really just a kind of specialized expert system that deals with databases accessible through computer networks.

Carmen: Are knowbots intelligent, then?

David: No, certainly not intelligent in the sense that a human is intelligent. However, they can transmit, transform, and store immense amounts of data. Knowbots developed inevitably from the point when computers were networked together and used to store large distributed databases. You need tools similar to knowbots in order to gather and organize information from computer networks. Knowbots grew out of a combination of ideas from network bulletin boards, electronic mail systems, and expert systems.

Carmen: Show me the one you made for Tamara.

David: Do you see this cluster of text windows in the holographic display? That's the knowbot. This window displays all the information on Tamara's query request, starting with the sentence she typed in which framed her information need: "I am writing a doctoral thesis on the historical development of the concept of human rights, with a focus on the philosophical doctrine of heterotelism, and I want to review the literature on the subject."

Carmen: It can understand sentences?

David: The knowbot has a natural language parser, or program to break down sentences into components which it can analyze. It prompts you with yes or no questions to make sure it has analyzed your query correctly. As I said before, it's important to remember that it really is not intelligent. It can only apply its rules of programming to your query. We refined the query in various ways as we went along, but we started out with Tamara's sentence.

Carmen: I think I understand. What happened then?

David: Then we went to the window of the knowbot which governs network operations, and typed in where we wanted the knowbot to search. You can either type in the identifying names for specific databases, or pick them from a pop up menu. Based on topical focus and journal coverage, Tamara and I picked out five databases that we thought would give us the best results. If we had wanted to, we could have picked clusters of databases or entire regions of the network. You usually don't want to tell the knowbot to search entire network regions because of the cost involved in searching through so much data. That brings us to another very important piece of

146 THINKING ROBOTS . . .

information that goes in the network window, the knowbot's operating budget.

Carmen: What? I have to put it on a budget, like my husband?

David: You sure do. When the knowbot is activated, it will connect to the network systems that you have chosen, translate your query into executable searches on those systems according to their protocols, gather information, and collect it on your workstation. Most of the network databases that you will typically want to search are commercial repositories of information and charge fees for providing your knowbot with information. Your knowbot has to know how much money you want to spend on the search!

Carmen: But how on earth would I know how much money would be needed or reasonable to spend?

David: The knowbot has current information about the fee schedules of different database systems and can estimate the cost of a given query. In other words, it can tell you about how much the search will cost.

Carmen: Hmm. But since we're searching so many different databases at once, won't the costs of retrieving all those articles and citations be astronomical?

David: Not at all, because at this point we aren't retrieving the actual information yet, just information about the information!

Carmen: That sounds like it would cost even more money.

Tamara: No, it's like asking a store for a catalog of their merchandise. You haven't bought anything yet, you're just trying to find out if they have anything you want.

David: Right. They may still charge you for the catalog, but not a great deal. After all, they want you to see all the great things they have to offer.

Carmen: Okay. So then what happens?

David: The knowbot "looks through the catalogs." It compares the query you gave it to the documents in the various databases. It finds the documents which are the most similar to your query in statistical terms. It ranks them in descending order and, depending on how much budget it has left, retrieves as many as are affordable of the top candidate documents. These will be the items that are most likely to be relevant to your needs and not just any citations which happen to contain a few keywords you entered.

Tamara: It produces great results. The first time we did a search we retrieved and printed out the top 50 hits. Almost all of them were exactly on my topic. We told the knowbot which ones I liked best. We also told the knowbot about some that weren't useful to me.

David: That's right. An important part of using knowbots for searching is that you can refine the knowbot's understanding of your information needs. After we picked the top five and the worst five items in the first list it retrieved for Tamara, it used the information to statistically modify its profile of her query. After that it didn't make any mistakes that we noticed in ranking its output.

Carmen: That's quite impressive. Now I have a better idea of what you're talking about. But you still haven't explained what a "similarity space" is.

David: One of the things that the knowbot can do is feed data into another specialized program that can graphically represent the characteristics of the databases the knowbot has explored. Graphical representations can show you patterns in the literature that are useful for the researcher to know about. A graphical representation of the similarity relationships of documents in a database is called a SSV for similarity space visualization, or simspace for short. It's a "space" in the sense that the statistical measurements of similarity between documents are represented by spatial relationships. A SSV typically looks like zillions of multicolored dots clustered in clouds or surface shapes. Each dot represents a document in the database. For any given document, the neighboring dots will be other documents that are statistically similar to it. The colors, heights from the surface plane, and other aspects of the graphics can represent other data, but the main idea is that documents that are similar in concepts will be close spatially. Let me reactivate the simspace associated with Tamara's knowbot so you can see an example.

Carmen: It certainly is colorful.

Tamara: I think these simspace graphics are beautiful.

David: I find the simspace visualizer fun to work with, because it can transform an enormous amount of data into gorgeous patterns that you can grasp intuitively.

Carmen: So these "planets" are databases indexing different kinds of literature. What a strange concept.

David: The visualizer can represent the similarity data in lots of ways. Those spheres are representations of the five databases that Tamara and I decided to explore. Each representation is a simspace normalized or "mapped" onto a sphere. Some of the spheres are bigger than others because they have more documents than others. Color and "altitude" on the surfaces of the simspace spheres indicates relevance to Tamara's query. Let's take a closer look at one of these simspaces, the little one there that sort of looks like Mars.

Carmen: Hmph. Those other spheres that look like gas giants must contain some of my colleagues' work. You use a joystick to move the view around? I thought joysticks were just for video games.

David: Video games usually involve a lot of three dimensional movement, and most people are accustomed to using joysticks in that context. We use joysticks when working with simspaces because they are an effective control device. It is sort of fun though, too....

Tamara: Yes, the effect is like flying a spacecraft down to the simspace planets.

David: Would you like to "fly" it, Dr. Rodriguez?

Carmen: Well, now that you've offered, yes! It looks intriguing. How do I make it work?

David: That slider controls your "speed." The joystick handles just like a video game aircraft. See if you can maneuver the view down to the surface of the red "planet."

Carmen: This is fun. Hmm. The surface detail is incredible. What are all the red continents with spiky mountains? This "planet" is actually a database, right?

David: Right, you're currently cruising over the "surface" of *Philosopher's Index*, a database published in Bowling Green, Ohio. The "mountainous regions" are clusters of documents that are more akin to Tamara's research interests than the surrounding "plains." Fly in closer to that region of peaks.

Carmen: The one with the blinking lights? What is that, anyway, a colony?

David: Sort of. Quit laughing, Tamara. Those blinking lights at the peaks are the documents that Tamara retrieved during her first search. The visualizer marks them for future reference.

Carmen: Why are the mountains red, and the flatlands green and blue?

David: When I asked Tamara how to color the landscape, she picked a spectrum in which red means "most relevant" on one end, and blue means "least relevant" on the other end. The color is just another way of viewing the relationships in the database. Red mountains are what she wanted to look for. You could just as easily reverse the graphical representation so that the most relevant regions of the database showed up as purple valleys.

Carmen: Hmm, let me see if I can "land" this spaceship of the mind. Hey! Now that we're near the surface I can see all kinds of ... objects? What are those things, trees or what?

David: The visualizer is programmed to represent some kinds of documents in special ways to distinguish them. The "trees," as you call them, in this simspace represent review articles. Critiques, overview articles, and other identifiable classes of documents are represented by other distinctive shapes.

Carmen: I see. So how do I actually retrieve one of these documents if I want to read it?

David: Hold down this button on the stick and cross hairs will appear. Center the cross hairs on a surface object, pull the trigger and the system will retrieve the text of that item from the database.

Carmen: Fascinating. So I could investigate why this entire ridge of spiked shrubs is so reddish and therefore relevant to Tamara's needs presumably?

David: Exactly.

Carmen: Let me try the trigger. I wish I could shoot down the arguments of some philosophers this easily. Interesting! This window that's popped up contains ... what, a citation and abstract?

David: Right. It's from a colloquium on heterotelism, Tamara's main topic of interest. The "shrubs" as you call them must all be citations to articles from this colloquium.

Tamara: And now that spot shows a blinking light, like the others I've looked at. I really think this search will help my thesis a lot.

Carmen: It certainly livens up the process of scholarly research. It also poses an ethical question.

David: What's that?

Carmen: This holographic workstation looks pretty expensive. Businesses, research centers, and rich universities like ours may be able to afford this kind of gadget, but what about the average people on the street? When do they get to explore similarity space?

David: You have a very good point there. It's the old question of the information haves and have nots. Information technology is only liberating for those who have access to it.

Tamara: I never thought of that. Now I feel kind of guilty sitting here using this computer.

David: There are a lot of other ethical questions raised by new systems like this. It's easier than ever to pirate information. The database vendors lose a lot of money to software pirates who use knowbots to illegally copy similarity spaces, falsify account information, and other shady activities.

Carmen: I suppose Pandora's technology box never gives you uncomplicated gifts.

Tamara: Well, I still like the searching I can do on this workstation.

Carmen: I have to admit, I find the possibilities fascinating. Has anyone used similarity spaces to study patterns of scholarly research and activity? It strikes me that you could use these visualizations to study all kinds of patterns in the literature. For instance, does a paradigm shift look like a cresting wave on a simspace beach?

David: Now you're beyond my expertise. Why don't you log on and find out?

Notes

The idea of similarity spaces was inspired by a presentation by Scott Deerwester at the 1991 annual conference of the American Library Association. His presentation involved the use of a NeXT workstation to graphically show clustering properties of citations in terms of similarity. Although he did not use the term "similarity space," and his graphical representations were not much like what I have described in this dialog, his presentation nevertheless inspired in me the strong belief that graphical representations of database properties are a wave of the future.

For an excellent discussion of the general concept of similarity space (the more traditional term in information retrieval research is "Vector Space") see the classic textbook *Automatic Text Processing* by Gerard Salton (Reading, Mass.: AddisonWesley, 1988), chapter 10.

For a more abstracted and advanced discussion of the problems of similarity analysis, see the book *Multidimensional Similarity Structure Analysis* by Ingwer Borg and James Lingoes (New York: SpringerVerlag, 1987).

Martin Halbert is Automation and Reference Librarian at the Fondren Library of Rice University in Houston, Texas. Internet: halbert@ricevm1.rice.edu

A Day in the Life of Mr. D

Eric Lease Morgan

North Carolina State University Libraries

Mr. D is particularly adept at retrieving, organizing, storing, and disseminating information. Depending on the type of information, he is pretty good at evaluating it, too. To say he is a wealth of information is an understatement. He has access to vast collections of published and unpublished materials in written and audiovisual form. His primary purpose is to bring people and information together. To this end he is also very good at remembering names, addresses, and appointments. Mr. D is a librarian.

He had been with the Reid family since the birth of Thomas, almost twelve years. Consequently, Mr. D has gotten to know the family pretty well. Mrs. Reid is a financial planner by profession, a strong willed woman with a systematic mind. Mr. Reid is an interior decorator and is more relaxed than his wife. Thomas is just a curious boy. All in all, the Reid family is reasonably normal.

Mr. D had been upgraded a number of times since he was purchased. There were the expected improve-ments like more RAM, smaller size, and faster processing times. His latest upgrade which enabled distributed processing was something Mrs. Reid hadn't banked much on but, once implemented, she was awfully glad the opportunity had come up. Now the entire family could have access to Mr. D's resources simultaneously, even if the family was remotely located from him and each other. She was impressed with the capabilities of this machine that was the size of a bread box with peripheral inputoutput devices ranging in size from a lapel pin to a chalkboard.

It was a typical day for the Reids. Thomas went off to school, Mr. Reid had a client to meet, and Mrs. Reid had someone coming to the house in a little while.

"Mr. D, I would like to read the paper now," announced Mrs. Reid. "I'll read it on the white board in my office." Immediately Mrs. Reid's personal paper was displayed on the large screen. The paper had been put together by Mr. D the previous night. True to form for the newspaper format, the information was ephemeral. It contained the news relevant to Mrs. Reid's profession: stock market figures, gold prices, analyses from the market gurus. The paper also included a story on the peace negotiations for the Lunar War. Since Mrs. Reid wasn't very interested in sports, the paper didn't include any of that kind of information (except upon request of course). The white board is a very large monitor. It enabled her to browse information quickly just like an oldfashioned newspaper.

Mrs. Reid marked a few passages from the paper with her wand, and then asked Mr. D for the mail. There was a thank you note from a satisfied customer. Mrs. Reid responded in kind and told Mr. D to add the customer to her Christmas card list.

"He has been added," replied Mr. D in his usual robotic tone.

There was also imagemail from a friend vacationing under the Pacific. The letter included pictures of strange creatures creating their own light and a table full of extravagant underwater delicacies. Mrs. Reid was jealous; she responded with a "visual raspberry" and a smile.

"Who's my first appointment?"

"Your first appointment is with Mr. T. Randolph Buckwalter III."

"When did I see him last? What did I recommend for him? And how well did my predictions pan out?"

Mr. D answered the questions and, at Mrs. Reid's request, displayed Mr. Buckwalter's portfolio on the screen in textual and graphical form. Overall it had done well but showed a severe decrease since the war began.

"No wonder he wants to visit. We invested too heavily in stocks. With the war, business is afraid of spending. I told him we ought to diversify more. Show me the prices of precious metals beginning one month before the war to the present." Mr. D displayed the information. Naturally, there had been a marked increase in the prices of gold and silver.

"I'll show him this and make a recommendation. Too bad, he could have made a killing if he had taken my previous advice."

After Mr. Buckwalter had come and gone, Mrs. Reid continued work on her essay for *Financial Planner's Monthly*. She had decided that she really wanted to be published.

"I marked a few passages in today's paper. I'd like to have more information relating to those passages. Who is this David Witherspoon? Tell me more about the business he started. Where is it located? Who's their public relations officer? Do they have an office nearby?"

"Here is a biography of Mr. Witherspoon. He has written a few articles himself. Would you like to see the citations?"

"Yes."

"I have sorted them by the journals you like to read, then by length and date. I can sort them in any other order if you wish. You might be particularly interested in the third citation. That article is statistically significant considering the items you marked from today's newspaper. I have also displayed the answers to your other questions, but I can not answer your second question, "Tell me more about the business he started?" Please be more specific. Do you want to know what products or services it provides, what patents it holds, how much it earned last year, what its stock is worth, how many employees it has..."

"Alright, enough already! I forgot you can't read minds. Give me a history of the company. That should be a good start."

"It is now being displayed."

Mr. D isn't really a librarian; he is merely a tool created by knowledge engineers, the real librarians of the day. Real librarians are people who are very good at two things: asking questions and finding answers. To do this well, they know about language and its subtle nuances. They know people do not always ask for what they want or that they ask for something that will not really satisfy their information need. Once questions have been formulated, librarians can begin to find answers because they know how information is organized and where it is located. They also know different answers will satisfy the needs of different people even if the questions are the same. This is because people's knowledge bases are different. The question, "What is a financial planner?" asked by Thomas would be answered quite differently for Mrs. Reid. With these things in mind and the knowledge gained from experience, librarians can provide information better suited to the needs of individuals. In short, librarians create models of information storage and retrieval. They then incorporate these models into tools like Mr. D. In turn, these tools are used by people to help them with their everyday information needs.

By now Mrs. Reid's screen was full of names, addresses, photographs, biographies, graphs, citations, abstracts, and paragraphs upon paragraphs of other types of information. Mr. D had marked in red the items he was taught to bring to Mrs. Reid's attention: text from previous searches, highs and lows in prices, dates marking the beginning and ending of projects. Mrs.

Reid marked a few things on her own. She clipped and glued pieces of information here and there. She added her own ideas in between. Her paper was coming together.

~~~~~~

Meanwhile Mr. Reid was with his second client of the day at the Russell house. Mrs. Russell was a fussy woman with nothing else to do but redecorate every six months. Mr. Reid didn't mind the steady business.

"Good afternoon, Mrs. Russell. I understand we'll be redoing your living room."

"Yes. I'm having a very important gettogether in a couple of weeks, and the current situation just won't do."

"We'll see what we can do."

Mr. Reid took out his pocket version of Mr. D and used him to take a threedimensional picture of the living room. They then sat down and got to work.

"What exactly did you want to change?"

"I want to keep the same furnishings but the colors and textures are all wrong."

"Okay." Mr. Reid began by bringing up his catalog of fabrics and asked if anything struck Mrs. Russell's fancy. She pointed to a few things. Meanwhile Mr. D began to develop an idea of what she wanted.

"Oh, that one is absolutely marvelous. Can I feel it?"

"Sure." Mr. Reid pulled out his tactile gloves and gave them to Mrs. Russell. As she rubbed her hands together she could "feel" the texture of the fabric.

"I like this one very much but the color isn't quite right. The pattern's a bit too busy. What do you suggest?"

He used his drawing and painting tools to edit the pattern. He softened some of the curves, simplified the background, and generally made the pattern simpler. He then asked Mrs. Russell about the colors she had in mind. Mr. D displayed monochrome, analogous, and complementary color schemes based on her answer. After choosing the color for the walls they were almost finished.

"This is the part I like the best," Mrs. Russell giggled.

After donning the gloves and some special glasses, they previewed the new living room inspecting every detail. At their request, Mr. D changed the view based on different lighting conditions: time of day, weather, season, artificial lights. Surprisingly, Mrs. Russell didn't want to change a thing.

"I'll take it!"

"You know we'll have to special order this pattern because I edited it. It'll cost more."

"Oh, I don't care."

Mr. Reid proceeded to place the order with the factory. He instructed Mr. D to check on the order daily. He also contacted the people who would do the installation and made an appointment for Mrs. Russell.

"I'll keep track of your order, Mrs. Russell. Call me if you have any questions. Just sign here and I'll be on my way."

She signed and consequently Mr. D contacted Mrs. Russell's librarian to actually transfer the funds.

As Mr. Reid was leaving he thought, "Another satisfied customer."

Thomas was on his way home from school when he decided to stop in the park and begin his homework. The assignment was to read *The Hunting of the Snark* and write a report about it. Thomas asked Mr. D to display the text where he left off.

They sought it with thimbles, they sought it with care
They pursued it with forks and hope;
They threatened its life with a railwayshare;
They charmed it with smiles and soap.

Thomas thought this was a funny passage and drew a smiley face in the margin. As he selected the word *railwayshare* he asked, "Mr. D, what is a *railwayshare?*"

"A *railwayshare* is a document representing part ownership in a railroad company, a share of stock."

"What's a *railroad?*"

"A *railroad is* a path for trains to travel on. In anticipation of your next question, "What is a train?," I have displayed minimovies of trains and a bit of text describing them."

"Strange that someone would threaten the life of a Snark with a railwayshare," Thomas remarked and made another note in the margin.

His brow became furrowed as he continued.

Taking Three as the subject to reason about
A convenient number to state
We add Seven, and Ten, and then multiply out
By One Thousand diminished by Eight.
The result we proceed to divide, as you see,
By Nine Hundred and Ninety and Two:
Then subtract Seventeen, and the answer must be
Exactly and perfectly true.

This entire passage had been marked by Thomas's teacher. He asked Mr. D to display the note. It told him to write the mathematical equivalent of the selected passage and to prove whether or not it totaled three. Thomas wrote what he thought was the answer and saved it in the margin. His teacher would evaluate the answer when the report was turned in.

Besides the teacher's and Thomas's notes, the text included the notes from the previous year's students. Consequently many of the words and passages were marked. Thomas could read what others had thought of the text before him. This was especially exciting to students who had older brothers and sisters; they could read what their siblings had written. The notes stimulated learning. Gone were the days when writing in books was forbidden.

Almost all text could be annotated. In fact, annotation was encouraged. It fostered creativity and thinking. But more importantly, it brought people together who had similar interests. This was done by leaving an address with the annotations. Then, when another person read the first person's note there was the opportunity for communication. This accomplished two things. First, it put people in touch with people, the true sources of information. Second, it created a new type of literature, hyperliterature. However, the reader had to be careful about hyperliterature because it quickly drifted away from the original topic.

Mr. D delivered an urgent message to Thomas from his father. "Come on home son. It's getting late and I don't want dinner to get cold."

Thomas packed up this things and started home.

The day had been a normal one in the Reid household. Mr. and Mrs. Reid had seen clients, Thomas had gone to school, and Mr. D had been an indispensable part of these activities. Even though the day was complete for the Reids, it was not over for Mr. D. While they were getting ready for bed, Mr. D was busy putting together Mrs. Reid's newspaper, keeping track of Mr. Reid's orders, sending Thomas's report to school, and delivering mail.

As Mrs. Reid was falling asleep she looked back on the day she bought Mr. D and thought, "That librarian is the best investment I ever made, but I wonder why his name is Mr. D."

Melville Dewey would be proud.

Eric Lease Morgan is Systems Librarian at North Carolina State University. He points out that he considers himself a librarian first and a computer user second. He wants to discover new ways to use computers to provide better library service. Internet: eric_morgan@ncsu.edu

Symbiotic Cyberspace Libraries

Billy Barron

University of North Texas

The Need for SCLs
(Symbiotic Cyberspace Libraries)

Libraries of today have the problem that they only contain information written by a limited number of people. These writers can usually only publish on a topic in their field. For example, because of my professional background and reputation, it is not hard for me to publish on library computing or computing in general. However, it would be incredibly hard for me to publish on some other topics such as rock history, backgammon, or a fantasy book review though I may be qualified to write on any of those topics.

Another problem is that useful everyday information is often not easy to find in libraries. A personal example occurred a couple of years back when I had dried battery acid on a counter and wanted to get rid of it. Well, I thought about the problem for a while and realized that I had no idea what was the safest method of removing the acid. I was lucky that the person that I was going out with at the time was a chemistry major and knew the answer. Let's say I had not been so lucky. Reference librarians are reknowned for digging out odd bits of information like this, but locating such information in a library is still often an extremely difficult, if not impossible, task. Where do you start looking? None of today's catalogs have enough information to readily reveal any books or journal issues that would have the information.

157

What is an SCL?

The future could hold an answer to these problems through cyberspace. My vision of a symbiotic cyberspace library is a technological support system that contains individual bits of knowledge entered by all kinds of people. These bits could be accounts of an event, recipes, little "how to" tips, ideas for new inventions, opinions on political and other issues, etc. These pieces of information could be anything. The possibilities for the sources and uses of this information are endless, but a very important resource is direct data entry by the general public.

Ideally, an SCL would accept natural language queries and would respond with natural language and graphic images. The goal is to keep the SCL as easy to use as possible. It is an informational tool for the masses and needs to be directed towards them. The method used to store the information would be totally transparent to the person using the SCL. The user should not be concerned with the actual technical workings of the SCL. However, most users will care very much that security is maintained and that the SCL is reliable.

For SCLs to be really effective, a large number of users will be needed. It would not be unreasonable to expect that access to SCLs in homes will be as common as TVs are today at some point in the future. Good marketing of the concept will be needed for this to happen, but more importantly a social change will need to take place. Society will have to embrace computers and become comfortable with them for the SCL concept to take off.

Uses of SCLs

Historians could use the SCL to compile alternative views of history or to find little known facts about historical figures. Others may use the storage capability as a diary in place of the paper diaries of today. Reporters may be able to find more sources for stories. Attorneys can use these online accounts as research resources; it's conceiveable that they may discover evidence that they might not be found otherwise.

For recipes, "how to" tips, and the like, the problem of conflicting information exists. Going back to the battery acid example, it would not be surprising to find that some people would suggest using water and others would advise against it. The system will have to deal with such situations in some fashion. The best might be to present the person with all the methods and indicate the number of people suggesting each one.

Often I come up with an idea for a new invention, but do not have the knowledge, equipment, or desire to do the work of inventing it. When I come up with such an idea, I could enter it into a SCL with the goal of sharing the thought with a potential inventor who could turn the wish into a reality. Along the same lines, corporations could use the information to find new products to develop or come up with better ways to market their products.

People could input their political opinions on candidates and issues. Candidates and elected officials could use this information to better determine what their constituents desire. The SCL would be a natural source for polls regarding candidates running for office and issues, although an SCL poll would have the bias of representing the views of people who go to the effort to input data, i.e., those who tend to be the most vocal and the most technologically astute.

Additionally, the SCL will accept ongoing commands such as "keep me informed about new developments in cold fusion." The SCL will then inform the user whenever new information regarding cold fusion has been entered into the SCL.

Businesses might also set up their own private SCLs. In service businesses, repairmen could efficiently share experiences and solutions. The SCL would allow upper management to get a better picture of what is happening down in the trenches.

Security Issues

The security of this information is a very important issue. People will want and need different security levels. Security should be enforced by two different methods. First, there needs to be security on the information itself. Some information would be public and could be read by everyone. Some information, such as diaries, might remain private. In between, all kinds of different access levels could be given. At times, the person might only make the information available to the government. People might make information only available to colleagues or family. The possibilities are endless.

In addition to general information, there must be a concern for the privacy of personal data. Sometimes a person will want to be totally anonymous. Sometimes basic information, such as name and address, might be appropriate. In the middle would be only categorical data. Ideally, it would be best if no one including the system maintainers could identify who entered nonpublic information. This will be an incredibly difficult capability to implement and manage.

While this kind of system has the potential for great benefits, it also has the potential for abuse. Over the last few years, computerized analysis of consumer habits crossreferenced with personal data has lead to a junk mail explosion. Currently, data is gathered from all kinds of sources including the US census and property titles. It is not hard to see that marketeers will also want to use symbiotic cyberspace libraries for information gathering. Many people will feel that this is an invasion of privacy. In fact, recently, public outcry over such uses caused Lotus Corporation to cancel a planned CDROM database product of consumer information.

Symbiotic Cyberspace Libraries, unfortunately, can be used for spying and terrorism too. While I assume classified information would not be allowed on a public system, it is well known that bits and pieces of unclassified information can be put together to generate what amounts to classified information. The governments involved will need to develop policies regarding the use of SCLs by military personnel and defense contractors. It would not be surprising however to find that defense departments would have their own SCLs. Terrorism may have been too strong a word. A person or a group of people could enter false information into a SCL, either for criminal or mischievious purposes. It may be necessary to set up some kind of screening process or a method for some authorities to remove obviously false information when it is found. Perhaps it would be better to develop some type of accuracy score for all information. The accuracy score could take into account a number of factors including the qualifications of the person who entered the information and the amount of contradictory information already in the SCL.

Conclusion

Symbiotic Cyberspace Libraries have much potential for increasing the information resources of not only scholars and businesses but also the average person. Some issues regarding their use, funding, and implementation will have to be worked out. Fortunately, the potential for benefit greatly outweighs the potential problems.

Billy Barron is VAX/Unix Systems Manager at the University of North Texas. Internet: billy@unt.edu

A Clear Vision of the Information

Howard L. Davidson

Sun Microsystems Laboratories

The best window is one so clear you can't see it.

The purpose of library automation is to provide access to information in as painless a way as possible. Current speculations on how this process will be improved in the near future tend to center around faster database engines, more intuitive user interfaces, better ways of creating catalogs and search strategies, and ways of handling nontraditional information like images, audio, and video.

I wish to take a slightly different view point, and propose an "ultimate" library automation system. This provides a sufficiently distant viewpoint from which to examine what we can do in the near term.

The quotation at the start of this paper expresses the philosophy: the automation should be so smooth that it is completely invisible to the user. The information retrieval system that most of us use with least effort is our own mind. We remember things that we have learned in various ways and can see the relationships between all these different items with great facility. It is important to note that each of us has a very personal set of both the information and of the relationships.

If I posit two moderately extreme technological advances, it is possible to construct a truly transparent system. One advance would be a technology that would allow a direct broadband bidirectional connection between the user's nervous system and a computer. The other advance posits a computer with sufficient power to run a real time model of the user's memory strategy. A less radical advance for this model of the user would call for a data base engine with online access to any information sources that the user wishes to access.

Given this technology, a search becomes merely the activity of thinking about a problem. The interface will capture the intention, and the user model will decode it. The decoded clues will be passed to the database engine which will retrieve the requested data. The data will be passed back through the model of the user, which will place it into the user's mind where the user would have placed such data had it been gathered without any technological assistance.

The subjective experience would be like looking into your own memory for information and finding it where you would have put it if you already knew it. The dataspace can be explored in as much richness and detail as desired merely by exerting will. This is the first level of a proper interface to a library.

The second level deals with the problem of how to transparently aid the user in dealing with information that is unfamiliar or has no preexisting context. This is the usual problem we have when we first explore a new area. This breaks down into two large pieces: *following* the reference chains to all related information and *understanding* the information in its proper context.

I propose that placing both the article and the pointers to related articles and other forms of information at their "natural" locations in the user's memory lies within the proper definition of the level two interface. Actually understanding the information in its natural context does seem to largely eliminate the need for the user. Systems that truly understand what they are finding are true artificial intelligences as opposed to mere information retrieval aids.

At this point I expect many of the people reading this to have concluded that I read too much science fiction and that this vision cannot be attained. I will first state that even if we never realize this vision, it still provides a standard against which to measure our efforts. Second, what follows if a brief justification for my belief that we can, in time, attain this vision.

We are now at the very beginning of a technological revolution whose results may well dwarf those of both the industrial and computer revolutions. This revolution is our newfound ability to understand and manipulate biological systems at the deepest levels. This will provide us with both the engineering ability to grow direct neural interfaces and the understanding of the working of the brain that will be needed to construct proper "persona analogs" that can run in external hardware, or wetware.

One of the things we are beginning to learn is how the nervous system is assembled. A particularly intriguing aspect of this process is that we customize our nervous systems to our personal environments during the first two years of life. This customization is done by deleting neurons that are not needed to respond to absent stimuli. A well known example of this is the relatively low visual sensitivity of Eskimos to vertical lines.

The space that had been occupied by deleted neurons is filled in with glial cells. If we recreate the chemical gradients that guided the initial assembly of the brain we can, perhaps, induce the growth of new neurons through the available volume of glial cells to provide both input and output taps at interesting locations in the brain. This is a possible scenario for growing a direct neural interface without actually putting hardware in our heads. While I am quite sure that the proposed method will likely be wrong in detail, I still feel confident that with enough work in developmental neurophysiology we will be able to design a workable procedure.

The planetary net is well on its way to being constructed. Currently available technologies will be able to support terabit/second data rates in single optical fibers. Computational speed and storage densities are still rising at exponential rates. These existing trends will deal with the back end database problem.

The really interesting challenge is in the construction of the hardware substrate, and the software, of the persona analogs that will translate between our minds and the backend processors.

Even after we have managed to place an adequate amount of the right kind of processor in a handy black box, we still need to be able to extract and keep current the model of how each of us thinks, sorts, and remembers. The interaction between ourselves and the analog has many truly intriguing potential pitfalls. They range from avoiding destructive positive feedback loops to establishing the legal status of a black box that thinks like a human being.

Setting the technological details aside and returning to the original thesis, I conclude that developers of library automation systems should aspire to perfect transparency for the user.

Howard L. Davidson is Senior Research Physicist at Sun Microsystems Laboratories. He uses physics to make computers run faster and develops hardware technology for application in virtual reality. Internet: hld@sun.com

Ethics

Captured from the Internet on 1 April 1992:

> William Gibson, well known for his *Neuromancer* (which in 1986 antic-
> ipated what is known today as virtual reality), has a new book, *Agrippa*
> (*A Book of the Dead*), that apparently will be available ONLY in com-
> puter-diskette form, according to *Entertainment Weekly*.
>
> As reported in the *San Francisco Chronicle* (31 Mar 1992, p.D3), "Gib-
> son plans to infect the disk with a virus that will make it impossible to
> transfer the text to paper."

Disregarding the hacking challenge, the copyright questions,
and the worries about disenfranchised readers, did anyone
notice that 1 April is also known as April Fool's Day? Urban
myths are fun to think about, but internet myths can quickly
take on the character of reality with resultant network glut and
wasted time affecting thousands and even millions of people.
Good luck to you bibliographers out there who are willing to
take on the bibliographic ghosts.

... as for me, I'm going to be really mad if the first edition comes
out in a format that I can't read on my computer.

Thinking Robots
An Aware Internet
and
Cyberpunk Librarians

Crime and Punishment in Cyberspace[1]

Sonia Orin Lyris

Cyberspace is a computermediated place where people (or "inhabitants") can meet to exchange information. So any place that people communicate with each other with the aid of computers is a cyberspace. There are plenty of embellishments possible, of course: equipment that adds sensory experience and enhances realism (virtual reality) or that makes it seem that an inhabitant is in another location entirely (telepresence.) Today's cyberspaces are primarily textbased. Inhabitants "post" to electronic bulletin boards (bbs) or conference groups, send electronic mail to each other (email), and have realtime exchanges via computer chatlines (echat or etalk).

To outsiders, this sort of computerbased communication may seem little more than a quicker way to send written mail. But it is more than that. In cyberspace, information is the medium of exchange and an inhabitant's actual physical location is unimportant. So communication actually defines a given cyberspace community. Cyberspace communities have different problems than physical world communities and, as a result, adopt different rules.

Many of these rules are nonetheless based on the physical world's rules and are still under construction. Cyberspace communities are constantly trying to figure out the best ways to support their needs in a world of changing technology and diverse users. System administrators evaluate the practicality of enforcing appropriate guidelines for cyberspace behavior while lawmakers try to determine appropriate laws to protect against crime in the computer age.

---

1   Copyright © 1992 by Sonia Orin Lyris.

But what is a crime in cyberspace? "Crime" covers a multitude of meanings, from the complex laws of our legal system to the complex rules of social interaction. Cyberspace is a world with new rules and old rules and sometimes no rules. It can be a confusing place for a newcomer.

For example, we all know that it is a crime to steal someone else's physical property. But is it a crime to steal someone else's information in cyberspace? The answer depends on the location and type of information. For example, if the information is in a cyberspace inhabitant's private storage area, it may require systembreaking to read, which in most circumstances is a prosecutable crime. But it is not a crime to steal ideas, in or out of cyberspace. Since information in cyberspace is still largely textual, it is protected by existing copyright laws. But copyrights can only protect the presentation of an idea—in this case the actual text—and not the ideas themselves. Inventions can be protected with patents, but patents protect implementations and processes, not general ideas. Besides, a patent must usually be filed before an idea is made public.

So there is a great deal of information that is simply not protectable. In cyberspace, where information is easily and publicly available, taking, using, and even claiming to have created someone else's ideas is simply not a crime.

But most cyberspace inhabitants will not stand for it. In a world where every item of exchange is information or informationbased, inhabitants have a healthy respect for those who give information. People in cyberspace share and present information more freely and widely than in any other culture that has ever existed before and usually at little or no benefit to themselves. Cyberspace inhabitants share knowledge and information because it is an essential part of the cyberspace culture to do so.

So while there may be no laws to prevent someone in cyberspace from stealing someone else's ideas, when the theft comes to light, other inhabitants are likely to be unhappy about it. The offender's credibility will suffer significantly. This is likely to limit the offender's ability to get and give information. A good reputation in a cyberspace community can buy the generous effort of thousands of people at a moment's notice. Losing that can be costly.

Even so, there are many cyberspaces, and anonymity and name changes are often easy to come by. Strict monitoring of a cyberspace is impractical or impossible. At the heart of cyberspace "crimes" is misrepresentation. An inhabitant can claim another's idea as their own or can claim to be someone they are not. Scams, chainletters, and pyramid schemes are trivial efforts to launch and mass distribute in cyberspace.

What's an honest cyberspace inhabitant to do?

RULE 1: Know your neighbors.

Cyberspace is a large community, in which neighborhoods are built—not along lines of location, as they are in the physical world—but along lines of interest. For example, a conference group that discusses software engineering is a neighborhood of inhabitants who are interested in (and probably knowledgeable about) the topic of software engineering. In that neighborhood, over time, inhabitants will come to know each other not only by name, but also by the style and content of information that they present to each other. When someone who is wellknown and respected says something to their neighbors, their neighbors will listen carefully.

RULE 2: Read critically and crossreference whenever possible.

Cyberspace is very much like a living library. Books, essays, poems, and fiction are easily available, and the authors are often around if an inhabitant wants to discuss their works with them. But putting words in print does not make them fact, and much of the information available in cyberspace is based primarily on opinion. As with paper libraries, readers must read with care.

RULE 3: Verify the personal identity or reputation of your source when the validity of information is important.

In systems where inhabitants must use their real names or a traceable account number, forcing them to account for their actions is much easier. Those who break rules can be identified, and others can be warned about their behavior. But since many cyberspaces allow some or total anonymity, inhabitants can often present themselves as someone else. Even the Internet, the largest worldwide cyberspace, cannot enforce individual identification. Anyone on the Internet who has appropriate privileges or knowledge can create a new account or forge another name and account on messages. When the content of information is important, inhabitants need to make sure the source is reliable.

RULE 4: Verify the personal identity of your cyberspace neighbors before becoming personally involved with them.

While online, reading up on the latest technical writing conferences, Fred happens across Julia, another technical writer. They exchange e-mail about technical writing, and eventually include other personal information about themselves. Over time Fred becomes quite fond of Julia. One day another inhabitant tells Fred that Julia is really Max, and Max has been telling everyone except Fred details of how Fred was taken in. Fred discovers that Max considers the whole thing a hilarious joke. Fred feels humiliated, betrayed, and angry.

This happens repeatedly in many cyberspaces. Far too often, cyberspace inhabitants are credulous, believing everyone to be as honest as they are. There are a number of approaches to verifying the identity of another cyberspace inhabitant, such as inperson meetings, phone calls, personal references, and so on. Since it is impractical to take the time to try to verify the identify of everyone in a cyberspace, it is a matter of assessing the risk if the other person is not telling the truth—whether the risk is flawed technical information or personal discomfort. Friendship and information exchange are often closely linked in cyberspace neighborhoods, so inhabitants often establish significant personal ties as well as informationbased ones.

RULE 5: Don't be afraid to apologize publicly if you make a mistake, whether the mistake is technical or personal, big or small.

After Fred gets over his embarrassment, he posts a recounting of the events for his cyberspace neighbors, including information on the fake Julia and the real Max. Some fellow inhabitants are amused, saying that Fred got what he deserved for taking what Max said at face value, but most inhabitants are irritated. Some send angry letters to Max, and some refuse to talk to him at all. Max didn't realize his actions would cause so many people to be upset. After he sees the reactions of his fellow inhabitants, he begins to regret the whole thing, and even considers leaving the system entirely, or finding a way to get a new account and start over under a new name.

Everyone makes mistakes, and cyberspace inhabitants place great store by a willingness to admit them. Public apologies are fairly common in cyberspace, where personal cues are often easy to misinterpret. If Max were to make a public apology to Fred, most people would probably forgive Max.

RULE 6: Consider the possible risks and benefits of sharing information, but remember that in all but a few circumstances the benefits outweigh the risks.

Alice has a great idea for a new kind of cyberspace, but she isn't sure if her idea is *really* new. She considers posting a summary of the idea to the cyberspace conference to see if anyone else has heard of it before or can offer her advice for what to do next, but she's afraid someone will steal the idea.

It is good that Alice is seriously evaluating the risks of posting her idea to a public cyberspace, but she is probably worrying too much. If she posts publicly, other inhabitants will see that it was her idea, and if someone else should claim the idea later on, she'll have evidence of a prior claim. Unless, of course, the idea isn't original after all, in which case, asking her cyberspace neighbors about it could save her a lot of time and work. In any case, most ideas presented in cyberspace are not stolen. While ideas can indeed change the world, most ideas simply don't. Some of the best ideas the world has seen were ignored for long periods of time.

Impersonation and intellectual property theft are among the most serious of the cyberspace crimes, but they are relatively rare. Most people are not in cyberspace to engage in such activities; they are there because they want the exchange that cyberspace best supports: communication with people who have similar interests in an environment where physical distance is not an obstacle.

RULE 7: Expect to make mistakes if you are new to a cyberspace, but don't be afraid to ask for help or references from older inhabitants, who are usually glad to be of assistance.

Susan is new to the cyberspace conference group. She asks the group what their definitions of "cyberspace" are. Twenty people in the group immediately respond, telling her that this is an inappropriate question. They explain that this particular question gets asked every month by some newcomer, and while it is a worthwhile question, it has already been talked to death, and it takes the discussion away from other important topics.

It is easy for the new cyberspace inhabitant to be unaware of the serious problem of information overload. In cyberspace, more information is available than any one person can possibly assimilate. When information exchanges are free and spontaneous, some issues arise often, starting up discussions that repeatedly follow similar paths. In an established cyberspace with many inhabitants, some issues come up so often that older inhabitants become understandably tired of them. In some cyberspace groups, archives or regular postings discuss reoccurring issues for the benefit of the newcomer. On the Internet, this list is posted monthly and is called a "FAQ," which contains answers to "Frequently Asked Questions."

RULE 8: Remember how easy it is to misinterpret someone's intent in cyberspace. Stay cool, even if you're sure you've been insulted. If you must say something, say it privately.

In Joe's PC conference group, someone asks for advice on purchasing a computer. Joe posts a reply. Someone else posts a message saying that Joe doesn't know what he's talking about. Joe is irritated and replies to the posting. Before long the discussion has moved from technical discussions to namecalling.

Cyberspace makes immediate replies easy, so misunderstandings can quickly blossom into arguments. Because tone of voice cannot easily be conveyed with text, many arguments start up because someone attributes to malice what is adequately explained by poor expression or miscommunication. Substantitive and relevant discussion usually becomes impossible when these exchanges are public. These fiery interactions usually start with little misunderstandings and are often preventable.

×××

Cyberspace crimes are similar to crimes in the physical world, with the essential difference being the ease of obtaining and distributing information. Whether the information contains new ideas, poetry, opinions, hoaxes, or outright lies, the dissemination of information—or misinformation—in cyberspace is easy. This is what makes cyberspace such an unusual environment, with great potential for both sharing information and taking advantage of the unwary.

It is difficult to formalize and enforce rules in cyberspace, so cyberspace communities tend to construct and enforce rules that suit their needs as specific problems arise. Many of these rules are based on the inperson social conduct rules we are all familiar with. As in the physical world, it is considered improper to badger, slander, or reveal personal information about someone without their consent. Impersonating someone, or "blowing someone's cover" on anonymous systems (giving out names, phone numbers, and so on) is also highly unacceptable. Some systems have rules governing behavior, but such rules are hard to formalize and enforce. On one system, the rule is both simple and vague: "be polite." Surprisingly, it works most of the time.

Administrators who try to enforce rules often end up having to read a prohibitively extensive amount of text, and they are often forced to invade an inhabitant's privacy in order to be thorough. A number of law suits dealing with the privacy rights of cyberspace inhabitants have been brought to the courts. The bottom line, however, is that it is impossible to monitor all the communications between cyberspace inhabitants in cyberspace.

Between sheer volume and unbreakable cryptography algorithms, there is no sure way to know what information a group of cyberspace inhabitants are exchanging.

Thus, in practice it is the cyberspace community itself that enforces the rules, with the tried and true methods of the schoolyard: peer review, disapproval, and—if necessary—ostracism.

Since most cyberspace administrators are limited in their ability to hold inhabitants accountable for their actions, today's cyberspaces are largely run by educated anarchy. The biggest disadvantage of cyberspace anarchy is confusion; questions of proper behavior arise constantly and must be worked out among the inhabitants every time a problem surfaces. The advantage is that a more mature citizenship arises out of these efforts, one where inhabitants adopt rules because they work well and not simply because they are handed down from a higher authority.

When children play in a schoolyard they decide for themselves what the rules for various games will be, and they enforce the rules themselves. There are always bullies who badger or harass, but for the most part, children manage to interact with each other in ways that support the rules they have created. Children learn in a schoolyard what behavior works in a social environment and what behavior doesn't. If a child wants to be a part of a social community or an inhabitant wants to be part of a cyberspace community, each must learn from that community what behavior is appropriate in order to remain part of the community.

Sonia Orin Lyris has been an inhabitant of various cyberspaces since 1979. Formerly a software engineer and technical writer, she now writes cyberspace science fiction as well as fantasy and horror stories. Internet: sol@qiclab.scn.rain.com

The Canary on the Computer[1]

Steve Cisler

Apple Library

In Washington, D.C., at the entrance to Lafayette Park where tourists compose photographs that include the homeless and the White House in one shot, I met Robert Lansberry, an elderly man who was handing out a two page tract. The pamphlet consists of a single long paragraph of warnings about mind control, electronic surveillance, subliminal experiments, tooth filling implants, corporate conspiracies, and coverups by Congress. At the end is his address at a hotel for transients. He has been in the same place each time I passed by, patiently distributing his screed. Few people take him seriously (perhaps he should get a literary agent), but I think of him providing an early warning for the rest of us just as canaries were used to detect leaking gas in mines. Lansberry is a barometer of tension and anomie in a world of advanced technology used in oppressive ways:

> Electronic surveillance is everywhere. There is no way to escape it unless you seek wilderness. Almost all street lights and traffic lights are infrared TV cameras, as in George Orwell's 1984. TV sets survail whether they are on or off. Light bulbs in your home are TV cameras with silent radio voices. In prison, overhead light bulbs watch, talk, and hear all. Big brother is alive, controlling us, doing evil.[2]

His visions of the present are slightly reminiscent of William Burroughs' early work. His nightmare dystopia has driven him into isolation but not hopelessness. If he were without hope, he would not be sending out

---

1   Copyright © 1992 by Steve Cisler

2   Robert Lansberry, *Subliminal Mind Control in 1991* (unpublished pamphlet).

his long SOS in garbled code. About the same time that I took his broadside, I began reading less fevered, more traditional and scholarly works that question the effects of technology, the politics of automation, and even the philosophical bases for our beliefs in progress.

In *The True and Only Heaven: Progress and Its Critics*, Christopher Lasch points out that many people believed that progress was a secularized version of the Christian belief in providence.[3] Lasch believes that what differentiates the modern view of progress from the Christian view was "not the promise of a secular utopia that would bring history to a happy ending but the promise of steady improvement with no foreseeable ending at all."[4] The German sociologist Ferdinand Tonnies, writing a century ago, had a vision of the world as "one large city ... a single world republic, coextensive with the world market, which would be ruled by thinkers, scholars, and writers..."[5] Lasch writes about what he calls the "exhaustion of the progressive tradition" and states in his closing paragraphs:

> What is not so obvious is that equality now implies a more modest standard of living for all, not an extension of the lavish standards enjoyed by the favored classes in the industrial nations to the rest of the world. In the twentyfirst century, equality implies a recognition of limits, both moral and material, that finds little support in the progressive tradition.[6]

Most of the questions raised about technology and its consequences don't examine the idea of progress, per se. Instead, the critics say that everyone has to take part in the debate[7] and focus on the way that assumptions about technology are wrapped up in the objects. Langdon Winner says that the secondary and tertiary effects of technology are often more significant than those thought to be primary (saving labor, bringing a new product to market). The importance of the Industrial Revolution was the changes in society and not the individual changes in textile factories and rail transportation. He believes that much of technology can be antidemocratic.

> Many of the artifact/ideas prevalent in our time stand in flagrant contradiction to the ideology of modern democracy. That ideology holds that human beings flourish, achieving what is best in their potential, under conditions of freedom, equality, justice, and selfgovernment. In that light, societies ought

---

3   Christopher Lasch, *The True and Only Heaven: Progress and Its Critics*. (New York: Norton, 1991) 40.

4   *Ibid.*, 47.

5   *Ibid.*, 141.

6   *Ibid.*, 532.

7   Linda Garcia, "Assessing the Impacts of Technology," *Whole Earth Review* (Winter 1991).

to create social conditions and political institutions that make it possible for each human being's potential to develop. ... To a considerable extent, the ideas embodied in material things stand in opposition to the central ideas that we believe describe and guide our political culture.[8]

Winner calls for

- 1. no innovation without representation
- 2. no engineering without political deliberation
- 3. no means without ends.[9]

A more extreme view is put forth by Jerry Mander, Senior Fellow in the Public Media Center in San Francisco. He thinks that there is such a lack of alternative visions of technology because most of us live so embedded in technology (cities, buildings, cars, factories, computers, and electronic networks) that we cannot imagine life without those constructs. I can make it an intellectual exercise to scrape away the effects of technology and imagine life before electronic mail, before the phone, the trash compactor, central heating, on back to a world without inclined planes or cutting tools. To be sure, the amount of our lives spent immersed in technology has grown from one generation to the next, but it is not as big a change as he would have us believe. Mander says that the idea that technology has no inherent bias confirms our "technological somnambulism." He criticizes both the political left and right for believing that the problem with technology is who uses it and how it is used. He claims that the real decisions about technology are made by corporations whose profit motives are antithetical to a democratic society.[10] He does not fully substantiate his claims, so his handwaving has not convinced me, yet he does have a strong following in some circles, and the debate he has joined is important.

More moderate writers such as Winner, John Wicklein, and even Patricia Schuman[11] believe that technology can serve but that it needs watching, careful watching. Ten years ago, Wicklein published *Electronic*

---

8   Langdon Winner, "Artifacts/Ideas and Political Culture," *Whole Earth Review* (Winter 1991).

9   *Ibid.*, 21-22.

10   Jerry Mander, *In the Absence of the Sacred: The Failure of Technology and the Survival of the Indian Nations.* (Sierra Club Books, 1991).

11   Patricia Glass Schuman, "Reclaiming Our Technological Future," *Whole Earth Review* (Winter 1991). This article was reprinted from the March 1990 issue of *Library Journal.* It would be interesting to hear how her views have changed over the last two years, during which she served as the President of the American Library Association and dealt with a number of high tech issues such as NREN.

Nightmare,[13] detailing present and future abuses of communications technologies: misuse of personal data, wiretaps, surveillance of workers, unrestricted transnational data flow, and other unforeseen consequences of interactive technologies.

Library organizations have tracked and wrestled with some of these issues, but I find the perspectives from groups outside of my profession to be even more valuable. Members of the following watchdog groups have been involved with ALA programs and legislation in this area because they constantly test the pulse of the technology machine in this country and abroad. Over the past year they have been involved in a number of issues of concern to the library community as well as some that should be of more interest to us. What follows is an edited version of the accomplishments of the EFF over the past twelve months, followed by those of CPSR which has been partially funded by the EFF as well as the Rockefeller Foundation.

Electronic Frontier Foundation

- Inspired and helped to organize and present the first Computer Freedom and Privacy Conference. CFP was a four day event that brought together, in search of knowledge and common ground, representatives from computer networking, law enforcement, and privacy advocate groups. Cosponsored the 2d CFP Conference in March 1992.
- Worked within Senator Leahy's Privacy Task Force in Washington, D.C. in order to advance the concerns of the computer networking community in the formation of legislation in this critical area.
- Became a presence on the Internet with their node, eff.org, where they created an FTP archive on the net for documents on computer networking and privacy law.
- Testified before the Federal Communications Committee concerning the public access and design needs of the National Research and Education Network.
- Joined in an association with the ACLU and the Consumer Federation of America in order to plan and to act in the future to ensure broad public access to the information superhighways of the future.
- Launched the Open Road program in order to make sure that the needs of the public in the building of the National Public Network are addressed at the beginning of the project.

---

13   John Wicklein, *Electronic Nightmare: The New Communications and Freedom.* (New York: Viking, 1979).

- Began research and development into creating the tools that will allow nontechnical individuals using PCs to access the net over voicegrade telephone lines in a simple and straightforward fashion.
- Defined the problems associated with the questions of protecting nodes and carriers from unwarranted risks and liabilities in providing information services from the producer to the consumer.

The overall optimism about the technological future is expressed in their closing statement:

> The issues that those of us in the computer, telecommunications, and computer networking fields of endeavor can see so clearly now will affect every American and most of the people of the entire world within the next ten years. The opportunities are immense and the potential for an increase in human knowledge, wisdom and wellbeing beyond our calculation.[14]

Computer Professionals for Social Responsibility

Over the past year this group has become more decentralized with the head office in Palo Alto cutting back on staffing, the Washington office continuing its busy schedule, and the Cambridge office being established to direct the 21st Century Project.

> The 21st Century Project is a new national campaign to redirect science and technology policy in the United States to peaceful and productive uses. The 21st Century Project is a coalition of technologists, scientists, citizens, and policy makers dedicated to informing the public about alternatives in the deployment of science and technology in the modern world. The 21st Century Project is a challenge to the longstanding and continuing military dominance of science and technology in the United States. The 21st Century Project is an attempt to reassert a positive role for science and technology in the improvement of human life and the preservation of environmental quality. Gary Chapman, coordinator of The 21st Century Project, can be reached at 19 Garden Street, Cambridge, MA 02138. Telephone (617) 4977440. Internet address: chapman@saffron.lcs.mit.edu.

Marc Rotenberg heads the Washington office. Some of their activities have been run closely with the EFF; others follow a different path. Here are some of the more recent ones:

- Caller ID and communications privacy
- Oversight of computer security and national cryptography policy
- Opposing poorly conceived computer crime legislation

---

14   "About EFF," FTP archive eff.org.

- Network meeting and political association: uncovered FBI policies regarding the monitoring of electronic bulletin boards on a case by case basis
- Lotus Marketplace: helped force the withdrawal of the residential database while the business database spun off to another company
- Efforts to control the misuse of the social security number: worked with states and some universities on alternate forms of identification
- Support of international privacy efforts: helped coordinate the Privacy International group
- Promotion of information access: continued efforts to increase access to government information
- Public education: CPSR held three roundtables at the Carnegie Endowment for International Peace in Washington on civilizing cyberspace. CPSR organized the first public policy conference on cryptography policy in Washington, DC June 1991. CPSR also worked with Riley Information Services to host the first Electronic Democracy Conferences in Washington and Ottawa.
- Litigation: this could be the topic of a separate paper. CPSR has filed Freedom of Information Act requests from the FBI, Secret Service, DOD, NIST and is involved in litigation in a number of cases related to the previously noted issues. For more information contact Marc Rotenberg, Computer Professionals for Social Responsibility, 666 Pennsylvania Avenue, Washington, DC 20003 (202) 547-5482; Internet: rotenberg@washofc.cpsr.org.

Conclusion

What differentiates these groups from some others that question or oppose some or many uses of technology is that EFF and CPSR are immersed in the technology themselves. They make effective use of the computer networks within their own organization and in the research and industrial communities in the U.S. and abroad. Their offices are automated, and they share a common tongue with those who do make policy and effect changes in the high technology industries.

To return to Robert Lansbury, the electronic Paul Revere of Lafayette Park I mentioned at the beginning, his unfocused approach did reach me, but generally I would recommend trying to target efforts and activities through specific groups such as the ones I described. Whether ALA needs more activity in this area is up to the membership. As the end of the millenium approaches, there will probably be a greater irrational concern with the role of technology, but the number of reasoned treatises will grow as well as more fanciful science fiction titles. High tech advances and incursions into more and more lives will foment legislation, creative speculation, and action, as well as increased market activity. Librarians will continue to sort, save, disseminate, and generate some of this information.

Steve Cisler is a Senior Scientist in the Apple Computer, Inc. corporate library where he works with the Apple Library of Tomorrow program, the Apple Library Users Group, and information retrieval projects within the company. Internet: sac@apple.com

Ethics and the Electronic Society

Florence Mason

F. Mason & Associates

There is growing attention to the question of what constitutes appropriate ethical conduct for information professionals. This is sparked by the awareness that information and information systems create significant personal and societal benefits as well as raise new social issues. Censorship, conflict of interest, the individual's right to privacy, and equality of access to information illustrate a few of these current areas of concern.

Who Owns Information?

As the information sector diversifies, the distinctions among who is author, who is publisher, and who owns information are blurring. Societal expectations about the right to enjoy the intellectual efforts of others and the right to distribute one's own intellectual products are changing. The nature of ownership, patents, copyrights, and trademarks and the rights they convey are being discussed, and in some cases, redefined.

The Power of, or Control of, the Individual in the Information Age?

Who controls information? How are information professionals to act toward proposals to impose "paternalistic censorship" which aims to restrict access "for the sake of the public." *Prodigy* (commercial electronic utility) users recently experienced an exercise of this power when *Prodigy* "owners" attempted to control electronic mail message content by enforcing arbitrary rules and denying system access to those who would not conform to these rules. This case raises complex questions about who owns the communication medium and what are the rights of users as opposed to those of owners?

Wizard or Pauper?

Access to information defines access to resources and can enhance social and economic status. Information is becoming more important for economic survival in both a personal and corporate sense. What responsibility do information professionals have in helping or preventing the creation of a divided society of information rich and poor? Is it the responsibility of the information professional or is it society's role to provide universal access to information and information systems? In the case of costly information, will society have responsibility to subsidize access?

Your Right to Privacy as Contrasted to My Right to Access?

The right to privacy and personal liberty on the part of the individual is often in opposition to the right of the public or an individual to know and to find out certain information. Who decides how personal information is to be made available and used in our society? What is private information and how is it to be safeguarded? The ease of obtaining personal data reduces the privacy safety zone of the individual. Large personal information data banks simplify the selling, aggregating, and reshaping of personal information in many new forms unanticipated by the person who originally provided the information. Commercial practices continually challenge the definition of what is to be considered "private" information. Personal data is bought, sold, stolen, altered, exchanged or bartered, compared, and aggregated into comprehensive personal data profiles of immense interest to business and marketing concerns. In February 1992, the Federal Government instituted a ten state crackdown on individuals in the business of selling black market data from supposedly "secure" sources such as the Social Security Administration and the FBI (Behar, 1992). With the value of information increasing at the same time that it is easier to collect, use, and share, there could be a general societal backlash against all uses of personal information—by the government, by marketers, by insurance companies, etc.

On the other hand, how public should "public" information be, and what obligations does the information professional have to observe with regard to this issue? Government policies on publishing and Freedom of Information Act policies appear to restrict access with considerable resulting debate over how to provide adequate access to public information.

Creating New Information Highways or "Trashing the Commons"?

For at least the past two decades the national networks have been carefully tended "common ground" shared by researchers, scientists, and other users. As the "network of the people" grows, use and misuse of this "cyberspace" raises issues of user etiquette, norms, access, and legal rights. The workspaces of the national networks are increasingly vulnerable to the invasion of hackers and others with less than positive motives. New technological applications and users with differing values are creating a moral vacuum in which many rules have yet to be defined (Johnson, 1989). Will hacking, illegal breakins, and flaming close down or limit formerly open access pathways?

Man or Monster? The Mary Shelley Problem

Before long, information professionals may face questions already being raised in science and technology with the acceptance of invitro fertilization and genetic engineering. What is the appropriate role of computer professionals in determining how their work is used? Should they consider the societal implications of their work? (Rosenberg, 1991)

For instance in the nottoodistant future, could computer and information professionals collaborate to create a robot clone of a human being? Let's suppose they do and this robot does bad things and invades property or threatens life. What is the responsibility of the designers and the programmers for creation of this Frankenstein's monster?

Time for A New Ethical Code?

Information professionals have adopted various statements to guide the professional behavior. Some of the more well known are the *Code of Professional Conduct* of the Association for Computing Machinery, the *Code of Ethics and Standards of Conduct* adopted by the Data Processing Management Association, and the *Librarian's Code of Ethics* which was first adopted in 1938 and then updated in 1975 and 1981. It now appears the Librarian's Code is about to be updated again. (Finks, 1991)

Ethics is concerned with personal conduct and ethical behavior that defines a high standard of personal responsibility. Acting ethically means making decisions based on the principles of responsiveness, fairness, efficiency, expertise, service, and security. Ethical reasoning should make the professional alert to dilemmas hidden in daily routines and practices that are unfair or compromise privacy or intellectual freedom. Ethical principles, however, are not rules, they are guidelines which shape practice.

Advances in computer and data communications technology and their use are changing the information professional's role. Old rules don't necessarily apply and new rules have not yet been formulated or are not yet generally accepted. The pervasiveness of information technology strengthens the need for ethical behavior by information professionals. The sphere of the professional influence broadens daily. Many information professionals already have a broad scope of responsibility for varied types of technologies. A librarian in a medium size town might find her or him self managing an institution, a shared online network, a telecommunications system, a local area network, commercial databases, CDROM products, and a cluster of software products. Each of these systems and products have license, copyright, patent, and other rights and duties which define their use.

Societal expectation of accountability on the part of information professionals for the quality of the product they provide is increasing. Are information professionals liable for a security breech to an automated system or in identifying erroneous information? Unthinkable only a few years ago, the concept of "information malpractice" is being discussed in the literature. (Bloombecker, 1989) In a recent case, a Marine Corps librarian was dismissed after the crash of an A4 attack jet because he failed to update the maintenance manual for the jet. (Hotline, 1990)

One of the central ideas of information resource management is that information professionals must safeguard information in their care. Information is a form of property and must be protected. The problems of copyright violations, software piracy, electronic harassment, break-ins to data systems, and computer viruses involve issues of security to property and the exercise of appropriate professional responsibility.

Information professionals are increasingly responsible for data accuracy and service quality. Electronic media provides new means for publishing information and accessing information. Information professionals are often providing information direct from source where it was created. Formerly, librarians accessed packages of information which had already passed through a quality assessment process such as acceptance in a refereed journal. The profusion and diversity of sources of information further complicates and confuses this issue.

There is an escalating potential for misuse of information and electronic technology. Data banks and the data stored in them are valuefree; the intent of the user can produce negative or positive consequences. For example, in Guatemala, card registration from libraries was used for create assassination lists of the county's intelligentsia. In a different context, is it ethical for professional managers to read employees electronic mail in order to insure the employees are not using the system for personal use?

The economic nature of information is becoming a major ethical issue as well. Information can be used to create or deny wealth. Likewise, unfair use of information can be illegal and create enormous wealth. The recent inside trader cases illustrate this point. The question of how information is distributed and who get access to information involve basic ethical questions of fairness and equity.

Defining Ethics

One aspect of professional groups is that they espouse some form of ethics and define standards of ethical conduct. Adherence to a code of ethics is basic to the nature of being a professional. The work of information professionals, like accountants, psychologists, and social workers, involves making judgments which are unique, uncertain, equivocal, and have the potential of value conflict. In addition, information professionals draw upon theoretical knowledge and their training in procedures and methods in order to exercise control over a domain known as library and information science.

Key ethical principles vary little across different professions. Codes of ethics usually provide guidance on: responsible professional behavior, competence in execution of duties, adherence to moral and legal standards, standards for making public statements, preservation of confidentiality, interest in welfare of the customer, and the development and maintenance of professional knowledge. Of these, concern for the welfare of the client is paramount. Ethical behavior is concerned with the difference between helping someone versus not hurting someone. This principle is captured by the code of ethics of medicine which states, "First, do no harm."

Codes of ethics and ethical prescriptions also provide guidelines on how professionals relate to others. Ethical guidelines discuss relationships between the professional and his or her colleagues, clients, institutions, and society.

Ethical Responsibilities of Information Professionals

What are important ethics and ethical responsibilities for information professionals? How much privacy is an individual entitled to? Are information professionals responsible for providing accurate (as opposed to inaccurate) information? Do information professionals have responsibility to safeguard data and information? Do information professionals have a responsibility for their information creations, good or bad?

In trying to answer some of these questions, the following ethical principles are proposed to guide effective professional behavior.

Information professionals must exercise fiduciary responsibility. They are the trustees of information. The information professional must recognize that information is property and must be safeguarded appropriately. Information professionals must safeguard data and protect this resource when it is in his or her care. This fiduciary relationship extends to protecting against illegal software copying, to taking precautions to block unauthorized access to proprietary databases, and to vigilance against fire, theft, and virus attacks.

Information professionals must guard against maleficence. The ethical principle expressed here is to recognize the primacy of the welfare of the client, the "first do no harm" concept.

The information professional has a responsibility to provide altruistic service, to protect the welfare and interest of his or her clients. This principle many even extend to a generalized client, in asking what are the ethical principles that must be adhered to insure fairness to my clientele?

Information professional should provide beneficence. The information professional has responsibility to balance needs of different groups. The ethical principle is to uphold benefits for one group while not depriving or being unfair to another. In general, the ethical manager's actions should improve life for clients, employees, and the community.

Information professionals must observe the ethical principle of justice which considers how to distribute goods and services fairly. Under conditions of scarcity, it is an important professional responsibility to determine if it is more important to provide certain types of information than others. Also, are some users more important than others in their needs for information?

Information professionals must exercise independence and objectivity. Professionals must guard against improper influence on their professional judgments by vendors. The ethically responsible position for the professional information manager is to take actions and make decisions based upon the merits of the situation. The difficulty is avoiding conflict of interest and other situations where conflict of interest may be hidden or less visible.

The information professional must exhibit professionalism in knowledge and demeanor. The professional has a responsibility to master the complex body of knowledge which comprises his or her domain of practice. This is particularly challenging for information professionals who practice in a rapidly developing and evolving technical and commercial realm.

Information professionals must exercise moral judgment. In the case of the "bad" robot creation, adhering to a code of professional ethics is only a part of the answer. Professional ethics are intended to guide the conduct of the professional with regard to the client and in certain decision making situations. There are other ethical and moral principles which also apply. The case can be made that not only must the individual act in a professional manner in given circumstances but they must also be moral in their behavior. Creating a robot may have two orders of effects. The first or primary effect may only be a "technology substitution" problem. Use of robots could throw people out of work and deny them a means of livelihood. A second and more serious effect is the changes that the robot might bring to social structure overall, both in terms of values and to the basic fabric of society. Moral philosophy attempts to deal with this second order of effect. Moral philosophy extends our responsibility beyond professional conduct. In this realm, the creation of a dangerous robot is a morally repulsive act, and therefore it is not acceptable morally and ethically.

Conclusion

Codes of ethics define guidelines for making choices and considering the consequences of those choices. The rapid change in the information environment suggests that a new and expanded code of ethics is needed to guide professional decisions and values in practice. A new code should consider the way in which professional work is done and give guidance as regarding what kinds of action are right and wrong. Most importantly, the code should provide guidelines for justice, beneficence, nonmalefience, independence, objectivity, and professionalism.

References

Richard Behar, "Psst, Secrets for Sale," *Time* 139(8):42 (February 24, 1992).

J. D. Bloombecker, "Malpractice in IS?," *Datamation* 35(20):85-86 (October 15, 1989).

"Disturbing Developments," *Library Hotline* 9(37):1 (September 17, 1990).

Lee W. Finks, "Librarianship needs a new code of professional ethics," *American Libraries* 22(1):84-92 (January 1991).

Deborah G. Johnson, "The PublicPrivate Status of Transactions in Computer Networks," *The Information Web: Ethical and Social Implications of Computer Networking*. (Boulder: Westview Press, 1989).

Ronni Rosenberg, "Mixed Signals About Social Responsibility," *Communications of the ACM* 34(8):146 (August 1991).

Florence (aka Foxie) Mason, F. Mason & Associates, Dallas, Texas, is a consultant for long range planning for libraries. She is adjunct professor for the University of North Texas School of Library and Information Studies and is also adjunct for the Emporia State University School of Library and Information Management. Internet: 72550.2710@compuserve.com

Want to Read More?

She looked back into the room and saw Gentry pacing back and forth in front of his books, running the tip of his finger along them like he was looking for a special one.

William Gibson, *Mona Lisa Overdrive* (Toronto, New York: Bantam, 1988), 248.

Thinking Robots
An Aware Internet
and
Cyberpunk Librarians

Books About the Future

R Bruce Miller

University of California
San Diego

Our daily lives are increasingly interwoven with machines and systems that consume, organize, and deliver information. As these machines and systems become connected to each other in vast networks, new capabilities and influences are emerging that have the potential to completely change the very structure of society. Railroads, highways, and airplanes have each had a profound impact on society and, by extension, on each and every one of us. Those changes may turn out to be trivial by comparison as networked information technology pervades our lives. Numerous proposals are under consideration to build a networked information structure on the model of the highway system that could ultimately provide an easy connection for everyone to nearly limitless information resources. Fledgling artificial intelligence applications and electronic environments known as virtual reality exist today. Can you even begin to envision what might be possible? Is this a science fiction nightmare or a utopian vision? Do you have enough basic knowledge to make informed decisions to help guide the process?

The books described here are about the futures that could be. Don't be misled. This is not a list of predictions. These books describe what is happening today in laboratories throughout the world and provide a glimpse of some of the problems and the wonders that are on our horizon.

Don't look for textbooks or mathematical formulas here. These are serious books, but the average person can read and understand them. Many of them read like a really good thriller. Some of the very real science described here may far exceed the boundaries of the wildest science fiction! Even though a number of them are several years old, they still represent the most realistic and advanced thinking about the future. Read one or read them all. The promise is that you will have a better understanding of the forces around you and that you will be able to contribute to the shaping of the future that is promised by these advanced technologies.

Stephen W. Hawking. *A Brief History of Time: From the Big Bang to Black Holes.* (Toronto, New York: Bantam, 1988). 198p.

What better place to start than at the very beginning? Don't be scared of the title or the fact that this book is about quantum physics. It is extremely readable and makes even the most complex topic seem perfectly clear. Take the risk to contemplate space and time and the origin of the universe. You will be rewarded with understanding of how arcane physics research can translate into possible new realities. If we understand our past and can clearly see where we are now, even if we are still unable to predict the future, we stand a better chance of causing a desirable future to occur.

Sidney Karin and Norris Parker Smith. *The SuperComputer Era.* (Boston: Harcourt Brace Jovanovich, 1987). 313p.

The desktop microcomputer is most well known to the average person, but it can be argued that the relatively rare supercomputer—the most powerful of the computers—has had more profound impact on our lives. This book tells about the machines and the people who make them. More importantly it tells about the variety of applications that range from medical research to space shuttle design to animation effects that you see in contemporary movies. Incredibly the power and capability of supercomputers continue to grow at a fantastic rate. The capabilities of yesterday's supercomputers are now commonplace on desktops, and today's supercomputers will be rapidly eclipsed by what tomorrow offers.

W. Daniel Hillis. *The Connection Machine.* (Cambridge, MA: MIT Press, 1985). 190p.

This one is a bit more technical and is not for the average reader, but it is still understandable by a lay person. Hillis explains how and why he designed a new type of computer, the massively parallel machine. Envision thousands of individual computers harnessed like a team of horses to work on a single problem. This computer composed of computers has the potential to structure its own way to solve a problem. Who knows what possible advances in artificial intelligence may be developed by this type of machine? Consider the possibility of machines that can evolve on their own.

CD ROM, the New Papyrus: The Current and Future State of the Art. (Redmond, WA: Microsoft, 1986). 619p.

You've probably got a compact disc player for music by now. Did you know that this exact technology is used to store huge amounts of data for use in computer systems, for example, complete encyclopedias on a single disc? Do you know how it works? What do compact discs and bulletproof windows have in common? The book is a collection of chapters by different authors that explains in clear language how data get on and off a disc with examples of interesting applications and thoughtful discussion of pros and cons and other issues. Ready access to massive amounts of data is fundamental to the rapid changes in information technology.

Stewart Brand. The Media Lab: Inventing the Future at MIT. (New York: Viking, 1987). 285p.

If you read only one book from this list, read this one. The Media Lab at MIT has lead the way in research on the convergence of recording, broadcasting, film, and publishing with the goal of involving you, the audience, directly in the media. Play and learning are one and the same in the Media Lab. There are animation projects, robots made from LEGOs, holograms, "talking heads," and much more. The result of all the fun is solid technology that benefits us in very direct ways.

Howard Rheingold. Virtual Reality. (New York: Summit Books, 1991). 415p.

You've seen it in the movies (remember TRON?). Imagine being able to step through the looking glass of your computer terminal and seeing, feeling, moving, and interacting with a world that exists only electronically. The conventional rules of time and space are suspended. Powerful information resources are at your beck and call. Welcome to the world of artificial or virtual reality. However, it has escaped from the movie special effects studio and now has business, medical, and military applications. Rheingold provides a terrific guided tour through today's reality of virtual reality.

K. Eric Drexler. *Engines of Creation.* **(New York: Anchor Press, 1987). 298p.**

Drexler wants to develop molecular sized robots equipped with artificial intelligence that can be placed inside a human body to "fix things up." An injection of these robots could charge off and eliminate a cancerous situation. The miniature robots could then dismantle themselves to be harmlessly flushed from the body. Perhaps you could have one robot in every cell in your body with the job to watch over DNA to trigger regenerative activity to repair damaged molecules so that nothing ever wears out. In other words, you would be forever young. These robots could even be equipped to modify your entire appearance and to change you into another person on command. Impossible? Read the book and find out. Two thoughts to pique your interest: Drexler is a respected researcher who is actively working on these concepts, and there have already been numerous laboratory successes at creating specially tailored molecules to perform selected tasks ranging from cleaning up oil spills to use in drug therapies.

Grant Fjermedal. *The Tomorrow Makers: A Brave New World of Living-Brain Machines.* **(New York: Macmillan, 1986). 272p.**

Here you will find the best overview of the leading edge in robotics and the associated developments in artificial reality. As with the other books you will learn about amazing developments that exist today and you will learn what the researchers plan to do next. You'll discover some of the problems with building mobile robots and equipping them with enough intelligence to be useful, and you'll be entertained by the clever, counterintuitive solutions to some of those problems. The last part of the book moves from examination of the technology to focus on the potential societal impact and the ethical responsibilities that we have before us right now. Fjermedal quotes another of the recommended authors, Hans Moravec, "We are on the threshold of a change in the universe comparable to the transition from non-life to life." Read the book and decide for yourself.

Hans Moravec. *Mind Children: The Future of Robot and Human Intelligence*. (Cambridge, MA: Harvard University Press, 1988). 214p.

Roger Penrose. *The Emperor's New Mind: Concerning Computers, Minds, and the Laws of Physics*. (New York: Oxford University Press, 1989). 466p.

Robert L. Nadeau. *Mind, Machines, and Human Consciousness*. (Chicago: Contemporary Books, 1991). 247p.

The scientist, the doubting philosopher, and the pragmatic humanist: welcome to a serious argument about the future of humanity.

Moravec posits a postbiological society. Interested in immortality? Create a computer copy of your mind and download it into a robotic chassis. You could then repair or upgrade your hardware whenever you had the need or desire. Another possibility is an evolution of artificial intelligence to a level of self support in which humans are no longer needed. A good bet is that you think these are impossible ideas. Read the book and you'll learn not only that the possibility exists but that this leading mobile robotics researcher thinks that it could happen in our lifetimes. Some of the envisioned scenarios are more outrageous than any science fiction you can find. The scary part is that they seem so plausible.

Penrose is perhaps the most respected and articulate of the scholarly community who argues that the essence of humanity can never be replicated by a machine. In other words, "artificial" and "intelligence" are two words that will never properly belong side by side. His book is full of formulas and is pretty tough reading, but it is worthwhile to see how he makes the case.

Nadeau points out that the arguments about artificial intelligence have been going on for a long time and that they have missed the important point. It doesn't matter whether or not an artificial intelligence program has the potential to become conscious exactly like a human being. What matters is whether it can become so sophisticated in a world of evolving, self-replicating machines that this alien machine consciousness will displace human consciousness. If you take the evolutionary side of the argument, it is easy to dismiss the ethical issues. If you choose to argue solely about the replication of human consciousness, it is easy to dismiss the dangers since you can make a good case that it will not happen. If you care about the essence of humanity, you must educate yourself on these matters in order to guide the process. Change will happen with or without you.

Koji Kobayashi. *Computers and Communication: A Vision of C&C.* (Cambridge, MA: MIT Press, 1986). 190p.

Twenty years ago the dreams of machine translation of languages seemed to be disappearing into the future. Today, however, with the hardware and software advances that seemed implausible then, it is reasonable to think of instantaneous translation while talking to someone on the telephone: you could call someone in Japan, she could speak Japanese, you could speak English, and an intervening program would make sure that you both understood each other. Primitive systems that can do this (albeit slowly and with a number of errors) already exist. Kobayashi joined NEC Corporation in Japan in 1929 and led it to today. He shares his vision then and his vision for the future as he describes what it means to combine computer and communications technology.

Clifford Stoll. *The Cuckoo's Egg: Tracking a Spy Through the Maze of Computer Espionage.* (New York: Doubleday, 1989). 326p.

Are you interested in the resolution of a 75 cent accounting error in a university computer system? Me neither. However, Stoll's rambunctious perseverance turned into a major spy case that involved most of the U.S. military networks and an international spy operation. This is a thriller of the highest order, and it's all true. Even if you aren't interested in computers or networks, read this one if you like a good mystery story. What does this have to do with the future? Along the way, Stoll uncovered gaping holes in the security of all types of computer systems from financial networks to medical equipment. He discovered that our lives can literally be in danger from computer misuse, abuse, and terrorism thanks to exponentially increasing connections between computers. What is the future environment that will serve us best as the global network develops?

David Brin. *Earth.* (New York: Bantam, 1990). 601p.

Sometimes the best description of advanced technology and the societal implications come from brilliant fiction writers. Brin is one of those writers. He takes us to the future but one that is not too far away. His global computer network might seem like fantasy, but the reality is that it is not much different from the network connections that exist today for academics and other researchers. Read this novel and share his vision for the problems and, better yet, the possibilities of computers, networks, and artificial intelligence.

Cyberpunks!

David Brin presents a near vision of the future and individual interaction with information technology, but there is an entire genre known as cyberpunk that depicts a far direr fictional view of how things could turn out. These books are usually set in a decaying, gritty urban sprawl that bears more than a passing resemblance to the worst features of today's mega-metropolitan areas. Computer networks have become so pervasive that all computers are interconnected in a seamless interface. Virtual reality and artificial intelligence programs are matter of fact. However, these are not wild eyed ravings! In essence, these authors have mixed a few contemporary newscasts into a stew seasoned with the advanced technologies described by the other books on this list. The writing of a specific author may not be to your taste, so don't abandon the genre if you don't like the first one you read. This may be fiction, but the subject matter is serious. *Neuromancer* by William Gibson is considered by many to be the one that defined the currently popular cyberpunk genre; some of his other books are *Burning Chrome*, *Count Zero*, and *Mona Lisa Overdrive*. Rudy Rucker beat Gibson into print with *Software* and later followed with *Wetware*. If you want to sample a number of authors, try *Mirrorshades*, a collection of short stories edited by Bruce Sterling. *Islands in the Net* by Bruce Sterling, *Synners* by Pat Cadigan, and *Arachne* by Lisa Mason all take on the problems of a world in which corporate power supported by skillful use of information technology overrides no longer self evident truths and freedom. Cyberpunk writing is dark reading in a rough style. Read these and you will have a clear vision of some possible futures that technology could bring us. Then it's up to you to create the right future for our children's children's children.

The original publication of this article (copyright 1992 by the American Library Association) was supported by a grant to the Library and Information Technology Association from the American Library Association Carnegie Reading List Fund. This illustrated version is formatted as a flyer for distribution and is available from ALA Graphics (800/545-2433) as item no.15092.

Publication design and page preparation by Walt Crawford using the facilities of the *LITA Newsletter*. Produced using *Ventura Publisher Gold* (GEM Edition), Hewlett-Packard's LaserJet III, Pacific-Page XL PostScript emulation and PacificType typestyles. All typefaces are from Bitstream, Inc.

This book is set in Goudy Old Style, with titles, section headings and section footings set in Futura.